Robert Cormier

Banned, Challenged, and Censored

Titles in the *Authors of Banned Books* series:

J. K. Rowling
Banned, Challenged, and Censored

ISBN-13: 978-0-7660-2687-2
ISBN-10:   0-7660-2687-6

John Steinbeck
Banned, Challenged, and Censored

ISBN-13: 978-0-7660-2688-9
ISBN-10:   0-7660-2688-4

Madeleine L'Engle
Banned, Challenged, and Censored

ISBN-13: 978-0-7660-2708-4
ISBN-10:   0-7660-2708-2

Mark Twain
Banned, Challenged, and Censored

ISBN-13: 978-0-7660-2689-6
ISBN-10:   0-7660-2689-2

Robert Cormier
Banned, Challenged, and Censored

ISBN-13: 978-0-7660-2691-9
ISBN-10:   0-7660-2691-4

Robert Cormier

Banned, Challenged, and Censored

Wendy Hart Beckman

Library of Congress Cataloging-in-Publication Data

Beckman, Wendy Hart.
  Robert Cormier: banned, challenged, and censored / Wendy Hart Beckman.
    p. cm.—(Authors of banned books)
  Summary: "Discusses the life of author Robert Cormier, his numerous works of literature, and the attempts by public schools and libraries to censor and ban his books"—Provided by publisher.
  Includes bibliographical references and index.
  ISBN-13: 978-0-7660-2691-9
  ISBN-10: 0-7660-2691-4
  1. Cormier, Robert. 2. Cormier, Robert—Censorship—Juvenile literature. 3. Authors, American—20th century—Biography. 4. Young adult fiction—Authorship. 5. Challenged books—Juvenile literature. 6. Prohibited books—Juvenile literature. 7. Censorship—Juvenile literature. I. Title.
  PS3553.O653Z69 2008
  813'.54—dc22
  [B]
                                        2007028003

Printed in the United States of America

10 9 8 7 6 5 4 3 2 1

To Our Readers: We have done our best to make sure that all Internet addresses in this book were active and appropriate when we went to press. However, the author and publisher have no control over and assume no liability for the material available on those Internet sites or on other Web sites they may link to. Any comments or suggestions can be sent by e-mail to comments@enslow.com or to the address on the back cover.

♻ Enslow Publishers, Inc., is committed to printing our books on recycled paper. The paper in every book contains 10% to 30% post-consumer waste (PCW). The cover board on the outside of each book contains 100% PCW. Our goal is to do our part to help young people and the environment too!

Contents

Author's Note

I would like to thank Robert Foley, director of the library at Fitchburg State College, whose eyes didn't jump *too* far out of their sockets at the amount of material that I asked Jan Willett and him to copy. I especially appreciate Connie Cormier, the widow of Robert, plus their children, Chris, Peter, Bobbie, and Renée, for allowing me to attend the annual tribute to Robert Cormier and his works, organized by Dr. Marilyn McCaffrey. Connie, Bobbie, and Renée were especially helpful with their personal insights. Thank you all for helping me get to know Bob Cormier, the colleague, the husband, and the father, as well as the writer who asked "What if …?"

It is my hope that readers will use this book to add to their understanding of Robert Cormier, his books, and banned books in general. I have tried not to give away too many of the details, as that is part of what makes Cormier's writing enjoyable. Nevertheless, be warned—plot spoilers lie ahead.

Chapter 1

Battling Over Chocolate

A school librarian in a private religious grade school is presented with a copy of *The Chocolate War*. The donor is a parent who has not read the book but has only skimmed it. She points out to the librarian a page on which masturbation is mentioned—but not by name.

"Maybe I should rip that page out," the librarian says. The donor assures the librarian that she will not donate the book if that is going to happen.

"What would we lose if we take out that page?" the librarian asks seriously.

"We would lose about five hundred words on the front and back of that page that the editor and author felt were important enough *to pay* to have printed and bound in a book," the donor replies. After a pause, the librarian reaches a decision.

"I'll put it on a separate shelf for the junior-high kids only," she says. "If they want to check it out, then they have to get permission from their parents." Both the librarian and parent agree that this is a good compromise.[1]

The librarian's—and the parent's—actions in this case can be classified as *precautionary censorship*. Precautionary censorship can occur when a librarian chooses a less controversial book to avoid conflict. It also includes those times when an author chooses a less objectionable word or idea only because he or she doesn't want the book to be challenged or left off a recommended reading list.

In the example above, the parent who was donating the book was not objecting, just warning the librarian. They both acted, however, before anyone was given the opportunity to object. This gray area is one of the dilemmas that teachers, librarians, parents, and school administrators face frequently.

People who are responsible for the education and well-being of young people take that responsibility seriously. Part of that responsibility is using judgment to make decisions about what is or is not good for them.

When books are banned, the process often begins when someone questions if the book could be offensive. *Censorship* is the removal or suppression of information because it violates the standards of the person or organization that is trying to block the information. Precautionary censorship, as in the example above, is one type of response to a book that is questioned. *Self-censorship* occurs when a writer stops or is stopped before he or she creates the work. If someone else suggests that the book is inappropriate, then that action is called a *challenge*. *Banning* occurs when the book is removed from circulation—taken off the shelf of the library or removed from a teacher's curriculum.

What responsibility do teachers and librarians owe students and their parents to warn them of book content? What if that content might be offensive or upsetting to the child or might contradict the parents' or the family's morals and standards? There's also the question of age appropriateness. Juvenile literature and adult literature are obviously for different audiences. But it's not as simple as being one or the other. Within the "juvenile" category, there is a continuum from board books for the youngest nonreaders to books that are appropriate for mature high school students or even young college students. A book that is appropriate for an eighth grader might not be appropriate for someone in fifth grade, no matter how mature the child might seem. Some adults who have challenged books did so because they felt their children were being introduced to the book at too young an age, but they did not necessarily object to the book's being available for older kids.

Books can also be challenged for their content (for example, the plot or story line) or for the writing itself (such as the language used). Robert Cormier's books were challenged on the basis of both content and language. Offensive speech can be classified in many ways, such as language that is profane, racist, or obscene.

Three of Cormier's books—*The Chocolate War*, *We All Fall Down*, and *Fade*—appear on the American Library Association's list of books most challenged from 1990 to 2000. His books were challenged because of having offensive language and sexual situations and presenting religious organizations negatively (as in *The Chocolate War*), for showing that authority figures cannot always be trusted (as in *I Am the Cheese*), and for

Robert Cormier, author of many books for young people. His writing has won him accolades as well as criticism.

being generally depressing and pessimistic (as in *After the First Death*).

People have different ways of handling unpleasantness and negativity in life. Cormier's way of dealing with the unpleasantness of being a teenager was to talk about it and "air it out." Another choice is to ignore unpleasantness and hope not only that it goes away, but that other people won't notice it, either. Some people who have objected to Cormier's work did so because they felt that children should not be subjected to writing that made life seem too negative. Even people considered experts in children's literature don't always agree with each other. Charlotte Huck was a professor at Ohio State University who started the first graduate children's literature program in a college; she played important roles nationally in children's literature through serving on the Newbery and Caldecott award committees and being president of the National Council of Teachers of English (NCTE). Still, not everyone agreed with her when it came to Robert Cormier.

"Charlotte Huck wrote a scathing article insisting that Cormier with the publication of *The Chocolate War* destroyed the innocence of children," says Dr. Margaret Sacco, associate professor of education at Miami University. Dr. Sacco feels that the article was wrong "because we cannot protect children from the truth."[2]

Nonetheless, many people besides Huck objected to Cormier's work because of graphic violence, sexual activity, bad language, disrespect *of* authority and disrespect *from* authority. In Cormier's world, grown-ups will not always protect kids, not even their own loved ones. In *After the First Death*, for example, one man volunteers his son for a job that he knows will put his son in the hands of terrorists who are sure to torture the boy—which they do.

Some people pass judgment on a book without having read it. Just as "you can't judge a book by its cover," we can't judge an author by the book's coverage. When books are banned, a few words from the book are often quoted, or perhaps described without an actual

Some people who have objected to Cormier's work did so because they felt that children should not be subjected to writing that made life seem too negative.

direct quotation. Journalists, parents, teachers, and educators are often under time pressures and might not have time to read the whole book being considered. Someone glancing at a book might find single words that could offend but might not grasp the book's full meaning or value. In Cormier's case, as with many other authors, we do ourselves a disservice if we dismiss the book without reading it in its entirety or if we dismiss the author without knowing his or her work.

"We live in a less than perfect world," says Miami University's Sacco. "There are so many people that condemn books because they do not read them. They let others tell them what to think and just pick out words, etc., out of context."[3]

With books—not just books that are controversial—sometimes even avid readers don't know much about the author behind the books. Just as words can be taken out of the context of their books, books are often taken out of the context of the people who wrote them. Robert Cormier, as a person, was a well-liked, sensitive man. Even his harshest critics respected the man behind the books, once they got to know him.

First, his name: Cormier's name has been pronounced "kor-MYAYR," "KOR-me-ay,"[4] or "kor-MEER."[5] Cormier lived his entire life in Massachusetts, mostly in the French-Canadian neighborhoods of Leominster (pronounced LEH-minster). If he followed the original French pronunciation, he would have pronounced his name "koh-MYAY." So how did *he* say it?

"*He* varied it, too," said Dr. Marilyn McCaffrey, his colleague and friend, with a chuckle. McCaffrey is a professor emerita of English and guardian of the Robert Cormier Manuscript Collection at Fitchburg State College in Massachusetts. "But he preferred the French." Other New Englanders anglicized the name, and Cormier evidently pronounced his name differently depending on whom he was speaking with at the time.[6]

No matter how we say it, Cormier made a name for himself in insightful writing that readers—both young adults and not-so-young adults—might enjoy.

Chapter 2

Book Banning: A History

Book banning is not a simple case of the "good guys" against the "bad guys." The majority of censorship cases spring from someone's idea of what must be done to protect others. However, protecting people from harmful words or ideas can mean withholding information, even lying to people. It makes the "protected" people less able to make decisions, and it puts the censor in a position of power over others. Moreover, wrongs often have to be exposed before they can be dealt with. In 1964, Lyndon Baines Johnson, the thirty-sixth president of the United States, said "Books and ideas are the most effective weapons against intolerance and ignorance."[1]

The History

The idea of having someone in authority try to control what people read is not a new one. The concept is thousands of years old. In 360 B.C.E., the philosopher Plato wrote in his *Republic*: "Our first order of business will be to supervise the making of fables and legends; rejecting all which are unsatisfactory."[2] (Evidently Plato was not totally satisfactory to all, as his own writings have also been challenged.) Plato objected to some poetry because he felt that it caused "undue excitement" and

An engraving of a printing office in Antwerp, Belgium, about 1600. The invention of the printing press transformed the way information was spread.

that poetry should instead be dedicated solely to glorifying the gods.

Efforts to control literature in ancient times were more successful than those in modern times. Before Gutenberg's invention of the printing press in the fifteenth century, books had to be handwritten. If those books were destroyed (seized and burned, for example), there were few other copies around to replace them. For example, in 1644, English author John Milton spoke to the British Parliament to eliminate the licensing of books. At that time, anyone who wanted to print a book (the author, printer, or the bookseller) had to get a license from a government official. In what Milton called "Areopagitica: A Speech for the Liberty of Unlicensed Printing," he said, "As good almost kill a man as kill a good book; who kills a man kills a reasonable creature [in] God's image; but he who destroys a good book, kills reason itself."[3]

At about the same time on this side of the Atlantic, the governor of the colony of Virginia had a different opinion. William Berkeley said in 1677, "Thank God … there are no freeschools nor printing in this land, for learning has brought disobedience and heresy into the world, and printing hath divulged them."[4]

Another way to control literature historically and currently is by legislating what is allowed to be sent by mail. Anthony Comstock was an outspoken nineteenth-century Christian who was upset by what he believed to be immoral behavior. Two areas especially angered him: contraceptives and literature. In 1872, Comstock created the New York Society for the Suppression of Vice. He was instrumental in getting Congress to pass a law in 1873 to forbid mailing anything that was considered to be obscene or "lewd." This law was known as the Comstock Act. Comstock became a special agent of the United States Post Office. For more than 40 years, he held this position and is believed to have confiscated 120 tons of material. Although 3,500 people were arrested and prosecuted, only about 10 percent of these were convicted.[5] The Comstock Act says, in part, that anyone who attempted to sell or distribute any obscene or lewd printed material was guilty of a misdemeanor crime:

> … and on conviction thereof in any court of the United States … he shall be imprisoned at hard labor in the penitentiary for not less than six months nor more than five years for each offense, or fined not less than one hundred dollars.[6]

In 1914, Margaret Sanger, who is best known for her efforts to bring birth control to women, was charged with violating the Comstock Act for her book *Woman Rebel*. Many important writers' works were challenged under the Comstock Act, including those by Ernest Hemingway, William Faulkner, F. Scott Fitzgerald, John Steinbeck, and Eugene O'Neill. The Comstock Act was used actively until the 1950s to prosecute writers of material that some people felt was offensive. It is still on the books.

Anthony Comstock, who founded the New York Society for the Suppression of Vice in 1872, was a crusader against "improper" books.

Book Banning: A History

Censorship of adult books and other written materials finally eased somewhat in the 1960s and 1970s in response to the sexual revolution. However, at the same time, restrictions on children's literature continued to be debated.

Shel Silverstein was most well known for his whimsical poetry books for children. He, too, was not immune from the censor's challenge. Some people challenged his writing because, they said, it encouraged children to misbehave. In 1961, Silverstein struck back with *Uncle Shelby's ABZ Book: A Primer for Tender Young Minds.* (Later editions had the subtitle *A Primer for Adults Only* on the cover, though it kept the original subtitle inside the book.) In *ABZ*, Silverstein seems to encourage kids to take the definition of "misbehave" to extremes—but would his young readers know that he was pulling their legs? Here are some examples:

> *Uncle Shelby's Present: Kids! Clip out this certificate and bring it to your friendly neighborhood grocer and he will give you, absolutely free...a real, live pony.*

> *I is for ink. Ink is black and wet. Ink is fun. What can you do with ink? What rhymes with ink? "D R _ _ _."*

> *M is for money. Mommy and Daddy always fight about money. Money is the root of all evil. See the money. The money is green. The money is in*

Mommy's purse. Take the bad bad money out of the purse and send it to P.O. Box 42, St. Louis, Missouri. Then Mommy and Daddy will be happy.

Finally he ends with this direct statement to his readers, taking a stand on censorship:

Warning!!! It is not nice to burn books. It is against the law. If your Mommy or Daddy tries to burn this book call the police on them. Uncle Shelby.[7]

However, in all this fun that he is poking at his critics and censors, he has made a mistake—it is *not* against the law to burn books.

A landmark case in censorship occurred in the 1980s. Although the subject of the case was a record and not a book, it has direct bearing on the book industry. In 1989, rapper Luther Campbell, who went by the name of Luke Skyywalker, and the group 2 Live Crew released an album called *As Nasty As They Wanna Be.* Florida state officials brought suit against one store that was selling the records. According to the American Civil Liberties Union, "[The] *2 Live Crew* case focused the nation's attention on an old question: should the government ever have the authority to dictate to its citizens what they may or may not listen to, read, or watch?"[8] A federal district court in Florida ruled in 1990 that the album was obscene, based on the Supreme Court's three-part rule for obscenity. The court said that the work:

- was without serious artistic, political, or scientific merit;
- was plainly offensive to the community; and
- appealed to prurient interests (meaning an unreasonable interest in sex).

The ruling was overturned two years later.

In the 1980s, some recording artists had a "clean" version of songs that they knew would not play in certain markets with their original lyrics. Before satellite radio and cable television were prominent, it was easier to silence artists by refusing to play their records on the air. In the late 1970s, for example, in "The Devil Went Down to Georgia," Charlie Daniels substituted "son of a gun" for a more offensive term so that the song could get airtime. Live performances often used the original, offensive terminology, however. Luther Campbell had both "clean" and "dirty" versions of his rap songs, recorded completely separately.

With books, however, there is usually only one version. A publisher doesn't typically publish a "dirty" and "clean" version of a book. But some publishers have changed the author's work without his or her knowledge because the book was considered offensive. Such was the case with Ray Bradbury's work. For years, Bradbury's *Fahrenheit 451* was published in a "cleaned up" form. When Bradbury found out what his publisher had done, he forced the publisher to reissue the work in its original form. It is ironic, given that *Fahrenheit*

451 was about book burning and censorship. (The temperature at which book paper burns is said to be 451 degrees Fahrenheit.)

Now, in the twenty-first century, with the Internet and other electronic media, it is possible to get one's hands on most literature—once it has been written down by the author. However, if authors are themselves censored and not allowed to write, then it has the same effect as burning the sole, hand-written copy of a manuscript. Some authors stop themselves from writing something that they think might be considered offensive to others or might not get published, which is *self*-censorship. Ken Paulson, the executor director of the First Amendment Center, interviewed Judy Blume in September 2000 for "Speaking Freely." He asked her about self-censorship by authors.

"Self-censor[ship] is very dangerous," she answered. "And I think the more we are aware, as authors, of 'Uh-oh, this is going to get me in trouble,' it's dangerous." She noted that she was glad that she had written many of her books before she started to second-guess herself about whom they might offend.[9]

"A book that dies before it is born is the saddest thing of all in literature," wrote Cormier.[10]

The Process

When people object to a book, several things can happen. As described in the opening of chapter 1, often the first step is self-censorship. Teachers practice what could be called "precautionary" censorship when they choose not to have students read a certain book because parents might object to it. Their feeling might be based on their own personal tastes and beliefs, their knowledge of the community, or a history of that specific book being challenged. Librarians practice pre-cautionary censorship when they put a book on a special shelf—or when they do not buy a book at all strictly because it might offend someone.

On the other hand is the issue of selection. According to Justice David Souter:

> There is only so much money and so much shelf space, and the necessity to choose some material and reject the rest justifies the effort to be selective with an eye to demand, quality, and the object of maintaining the library as a place of civilized enquiry by widely different sorts of people. Public libraries are indeed selective in what they acquire to place in their stacks, as they must be.

Souter was writing one of the dissenting opinions in the Supreme Court case of *United States* v. *American Library Assocation, Inc.* That meant that he disagreed with the majority ruling of the court. In his dissent he further said:

> Selectivity is thus necessary and complex, and these two characteristics explain why review of a library's selection decisions must be limited: the decisions are made all the time,

and only in extreme cases could one expect particular choices to reveal impermissible reasons … like excluding books because their authors are Democrats or their critiques of organized Christianity are unsympathetic."[11]

The issues faced by teachers are slightly different from those faced by librarians. A librarian is selecting a book to be made available to a reader, who is making a choice whether to read that book, another one, or no

Librarians practice precautionary censorship when they put a book on a special shelf—or do not buy a book at all because it might offend someone.

book at all. A teacher is selecting a book that will be used as part of a course. The reader does not have as much of a choice as to whether to read it.

Sometimes when teachers recognize that a book might be troublesome, they contact their students' parents for approval. If there are parents who do not agree to the assignment, then their child is assigned an alternate. When that happens, the student is then left out of the specific discussion pertaining to that book. What might seem to be a good compromise may result in a student's being excluded. Many kids feel left out enough—especially as teenagers—without also being unable to participate in a discussion.

If a book is made available and someone objects to something in it and wants the book removed, that is called "challenging" the book. Challenges can be made in many ways. A parent might call the principal, send an e-mail to the teacher, or write a note for the child to deliver, for example. The process of challenging books is similar for both public and private schools, although the decision-makers might be different. In a private school, such as a religious school, a student's parents might talk to the principal or the religious leader of the community. In a public school, a student's parents might talk to the principal and then contact the school board. The principal is under the direction of the superintendent of schools, who is under the direction of the school board. The school board members are elected by voters in that geographic area—even if they do not have any children attending that school system. When they are elected, school board members try to reflect and represent the values of the people who elected them. They also have their own ethical and moral standards. Many times, the officials themselves also hold strong religious beliefs that affect how they judge a book.

School administrators, staff, and faculty members have to balance all these various interests in reviewing books. Therefore, it is very important for schools to have a written policy to help guide people through the process when a book is questioned. A written policy reinforces the responsibilities that these adults have to the children. It reminds them of the legal obligations and restrictions. It also keeps their actions consistent so that the same set of standards is applied in each instance. A written policy also keeps librarians and teachers from precautionary censoring if they can see that a text clearly fits within their school's guidelines.

Because not all book challenges follow a formal process, it is difficult to keep track of how many books are challenged and how many times. Joan Bertin, executive director for the National Coalition Against Censorship, says that censorship of children's books has always been common, even when the challenges of adult books decreased in the 1960s and 1970s. However, book challenges are increasing, especially since the 2004 election. During the campaigns of 2004 (presidential and others), candidates tried to convince the public that they were the best choice because they represented the morals and ethics of the average American. "Family values" became a focal point of the election.

"I've seen a dramatic increase since the 2004 [presidential] election," says Bertin. "Those who identify with family values feel emboldened."[12]

The Philosophy

Is it a good practice to warn people of something that might upset or be harmful to them? News anchors, for example, warn when an upcoming story might be upsetting. Our society has many ways to let people know about the content of movies, television, and video games.

Since 1968, the Motion Picture Association of America and the National Association of Theater Owners have operated a voluntary movie ratings system. After a movie is completed, a group of people known as the Classification and Rating Administration meet to view the film and recommend a rating: G (general audience—all ages admitted), PG (parental guidance suggested—some material may not be suitable for children), PG-13 (parents strongly

Like movies, video and computer games are rated according to how suitable they are for different age groups.

cautioned—some material may be inappropriate for children under thirteen), R (restricted—under seventeen requires an accompanying parent or adult guardian), or NC-17 (no one seventeen or under admitted).[13]

Similar ratings are used for video and computer games: "EC" is for young children ages three and older; "E" is for everyone (especially over the age of six); "E10+" is for kids who are at least ten years old; "T" is for teens, "M" is for people over the age of seventeen; and "AO" is for adults only.[14]

Compared to other rating structures, a system for warning readers about possible offensive book content seems reasonable and even responsible. Some books are labeled with a suggested age range. However, there are complications. There is no unique, consistent method for determining reading level.

One method often used by librarians is the "five-finger rule." They tell their young readers to count each time they get to a word they do not understand: If they reach five fingers within a page or a chapter, depending on the type of book, they should conclude that the book is too difficult for them. (It is sometimes suggested that younger children, known as "early readers" in publishing industry terms, should use a three-finger rule.) However, just because a student is able to sound out a word or understand its definition does not mean that content using that word is age-appropriate.

Other scales have been developed by both non-profit and for-profit organizations. These ratings are often noted only on the paperback editions of books. They are also inconsistent. A book for a nine-year-old might be labeled "08–12," "0812," "0709" or even "RL 3.1." As you can see, sometimes the number refers to age. Sometimes the number refers to grade level. Sometimes the number refers to reading level.

Reading level is not necessarily the same as grade level or even comprehension level. A nine-year-old in third grade might read very well and might easily be able to read a book written for fifth graders. However, he might not have the emotional maturity to understand the content of the book he is reading. A thirteen-year-old might have the emotional maturity of her fellow seventh graders, but she might have learning disabilities that make reading difficult. She also might not be interested in things typical for someone her age. So there is some overlap but also some difference between a reader's comprehension, maturity, and interest levels. Even if a teen is interested in a topic and can understand the writing, the content might still not be appropriate for that specific person.

Although confusing, the indication of reading level on the backs of books is usually helpful to teachers and parents who are trying to determine what is appropriate for children to read. Being a responsible parent means knowing what content or images are too difficult for one's own children to handle. But should one group of adults decide what *all* children can handle? That is the line between sensitivity and censorship. Being sensitive to *one* child's needs might mean not letting one specific child read one specific book. Censorship begins when a group of people is prevented from reading a book. In its most extreme form, censorship means saying that no one can read it.

Cormier wrote an essay that he called "Some thoughts on censorship," which he shared with many people. In it, he said:

> I sympathize with parents who want to have control over their own children. What their children should do, see, read. My wife and I exercised those kinds of controls. If parents object to their children reading *We All Fall Down*, I don't protest. But when they forbid other children from reading it then I strongly object. This, in fact, is the censorship problem in its most basic concept. Telling other people what they can do, see, or read. Invading rights of individuals in a free country.[15]

Unlike the movie industry, the book industry has never censored itself. However, similar to the Comstock Act, which controlled the mailing of materials, other laws control the industries around publishing. For example, local and federal regulations have been passed to limit the production and sale of pornography. However, it is not illegal for someone to read or own pornography (unless it is child pornography, which is illegal in all circumstances).

Among children, reading level is not the same thing as grade level or comprehension level.

Novelist J. M. Coetzee published a collection of essays about censorship in a book called *Giving Offense*. He writes:

> As a phenomenon, censorship belongs to public life; the study of censorship sprawls across several disciplines, including law, aesthetics, moral philosophy, human psychology, and politics.... The censor acts, or believes he acts, in the interest of a community. In practice he often acts out the outrage of that community, or imagines its outrage and acts it out; sometimes he imagines both the community and its outrage.[16]

Books are typically challenged for the following reasons:

- offensive language
- sexuality
- violence
- racial stereotypes
- gender stereotypes
- witchcraft or Satanism
- religious issues

Author and former public librarian Tony Greiner points out that public libraries and school libraries have similar but different standards—rightfully so—for what is considered appropriate or inappropriate. For example, popular magazines like *Hustler* and *Maxim* are nowhere to be found in public libraries and school libraries.

"Pornography doesn't exist in public library collections, unless written by a 'name' author like Anne Rice. You will find highly sexual portions in novels by writers such as Sandra Brown," says Greiner, "but straight-ahead porn is rare." Greiner notes that other matters, such as violence, don't seem to evoke as much concern as sex:

> Violence seems to be okay. True crime, graphic murder mysteries and "blow 'em up" action films are staples of public libraries, but overt sexual material is not. These are the community standards followed almost everywhere in the country, whether we like it or not.[17]

Censorship attempts and challenges increase as the audience's age decreases. This is not surprising, since it is generally believed that the younger children are, the more they should be protected from ideas and images they may not understand or be able to handle. Therefore, most of the books that are challenged are children's books. On the American Library Association's list of books challenged most often from 1990 to 2000, only about a dozen are adult titles.

The Law

As Americans, we are guaranteed a right to free speech under the First Amendment to the Constitution.

However, we are not guaranteed the ability to read and say whatever we want to in all circumstances.

The legislative branch of the U.S. government passes bills that become laws. It is up to the courts and judges to interpret the laws and decide how they will actually work when applied to real life. After a case has been taken to court, it is referred to by the name of the two parties involved. The first name represents who brought the suit ("the complainant"). The second name represents the person or organization against whom the suit was brought.

Over the last fifty years, there have been some important laws and court cases related to free speech and free press. Several key court cases have defined how we view censorship today. Some of these cases address freedom of speech in general, not just in writing. Some of the cases, on the other hand, do address the written word—both works published externally and work written by students themselves. What follows are some of the laws and cases that are important regarding what can be communicated orally and in writing in schools.

Tinker v. Des Moines Independent Community School District (1969). Three students—John Tinker (aged fifteen), Mary Beth Tinker (thirteen), and Christopher Eckhardt (sixteen)—were suspended from school after wearing black armbands to protest the Vietnam war. Their school district did not feel that it was an appropriate expression or that the school was an appropriate place. The Supreme Court ruled in favor of the students, holding that neither students nor teachers "shed their Constitutional right to freedom of speech or expression at the school house gate."[18]

Presidents Council, District 25 v. Community School Board No. 25 (New York City) (1972). In this case, which was heard by the Second Circuit of the U.S. Court of Appeals, a school board had forbidden junior high students to read *Down These Mean Streets*, by Piri Thomas, because of graphic sex and offensive language. The court ruled in favor of the school board. They said that it *is* the school board's right to determine that a book is not appropriate for a school library.[19]

Minarcini v. Strongsville (Ohio) City School District (1976). The Strongsville City Board of Education had disapproved

The Most Frequently Challenged Books of 1990–2000

1. Scary Stories (series) by Alvin Schwartz

2. *Daddy's Roommate* by Michael Willhoite

3. *I Know Why the Caged Bird Sings* by Maya Angelou

4. ***The Chocolate War* by Robert Cormier**

5. *Adventures of Huckleberry Finn* by Mark Twain

6. *Of Mice and Men* by John Steinbeck

7. Harry Potter (series) by J. K. Rowling

8. *Forever* by Judy Blume

9. *Bridge to Terabithia* by Katherine Paterson

10. Alice (series) by Phyllis Reynolds Naylor

Note: The list of the hundred most frequently challenged books from this period includes two other books by Cormier: *We All Fall Down* (#35) and *Fade* (#65).[29]

of buying Joseph Heller's *Catch-22* and Kurt Vonnegut's *God Bless You, Mr. Rosewater* for use in the classroom. They also ordered that the school library remove from its shelves *Catch-22* and Vonnegut's *Cat's Cradle*. The only documented reason for these instructions was found in the minutes to the school board meeting, where the books were described as "sick" and "garbage." The Sixth Circuit of the U.S. Court of Appeals ruled against the school board, saying that their actions violated the students' First Amendment rights to receive information.[21]

Bicknell v. Vergennes Union High School Board (1979). Elizabeth Phillips was a librarian at the Vergennes Union High School in Vermont. She protested the school board's removing *Dog Day Afternoon* and *The Wanderer* from the library and forbidding any new book purchases. (*Dog Day Afternoon* was based on a short story by P. F. Kluge, which itself was based on a real bank robbery. The short story was later turned into a novel and then a movie of the same name.) The school board objected to what they described as the bad language used in both books. The U.S. Court of Appeals for the Second District ruled that the school board *did* have the authority to remove the books and that it did not violate the students' rights under the Constitution. The Appeals Court upheld the decision of the District Court.[22]

Board of Education, Island Trees Union Free School District No. 26 v. Pico (1982). This famous case is sometimes referred to just as "Pico." School board members tried to remove books after a local conservative group objected to them, saying they were "anti-American, anti-Christian, anti-Semitic, and just plain filthy."[23] The books were *Slaughterhouse-Five* (Kurt Vonnegut), *The Naked Ape* (Desmond Morris), *Down These Mean Streets* (Piri Thomas), *Best Short Stories by Negro Writers* (Langston Hughes, editor), *Laughing Boy* (Oliver LaFarge), *Go Ask Alice* (anonymous), *Black Boy* (Richard Wright), *A Hero Ain't Nothing But a*

The Supreme Court held in Tinker v. Des Moines *that neither students nor teachers "shed their Constitutional right to freedom of speech or expression at the school house gate."*

Sandwich (Alice Childress), *The Fixer* (Bernard Malamud), *A Reader for Writers* (Jerome Archer, editor), and *Soul on Ice* (Eldridge Cleaver). A committee was formed, which recommended that five books be returned to the school library and two be removed. They couldn't agree on four others. The board then voted to return only one book, *Black Boy*, to the shelves. Students challenged the action of the board. After many years, the case finally made it all the way up to the Supreme Court of the United States. When asked why the books had been banned in the first place, the court was told that the books contained vulgarities. Justice John Paul Stevens asked the school board attorney why *A Reader for Writers* was removed, because it had no vulgarity in it. The attorney said that the school board felt the book was just in bad taste. Justice Stevens was shocked and asked if "bad taste" was an appropriate reason for banning a book. The Supreme Court ruled with the students, saying that the actions of the school board violated the Constitution.[24]

The Communications Decency Act (CDA). The CDA was passed by Congress in February 1996. The intent of the Act was to protect people from indecent or offensive materials that might be posted on the Internet. As written, the Act would even restrict works that had appeared elsewhere in print and were therefore already protected under the First Amendment to the Constitution. In June 1996, a panel of three judges in a federal court granted an injunction against the CDA. That meant that the Act could not be enforced until further examination. In their decision, the judges said that the Act violated the First Amendment as it might apply to the Internet. The case went to the Supreme Court, which ruled in 1997 that the Internet had the same speech protection as did printed materials. They struck down the Act. Chief Justice William Rehnquist and Justice Sandra Day O'Connor agreed that the provisions of the CDA were unconstitutional except as applied to communication between an adult and a minor (someone under the age of eighteen).[25]

United States v. American Library Association (2002). Congress enacted the Children's Internet Protection Act (CIPA) to protect children from seeing pornographic material when they use computers in public libraries. CIPA prevents public libraries from receiving any kind of federal funds for Internet access unless the libraries install certain types of blocking software. The court ruled that requiring libraries to use the software did *not* violate the First Amendment rights of library patrons. Chief Justice William Rehnquist concluded that "Internet access in public libraries is neither a 'traditional' nor a 'designated' public forum."[26] In his dissenting opinion, Justice David Souter wrote:

> We therefore have to take the statute on the understanding that adults will be denied access to a substantial amount of nonobscene material

Censorship Challenges by Categories, 1990–2000

1,607 books challenged for "sexually explicit" material

1,427 challenged for "offensive language"

1,256 challenged for material "unsuited to age group"

842 challenged for having an "occult theme or promoting the occult or Satanism"

737 challenged for material considered "violent"

515 challenged for having a homosexual theme or "promoting homosexuality"

419 challenged for material "promoting a religious viewpoint"

317 challenged for containing "nudity"

267 challenged for containing "racism"

224 challenged for pertaining to "sex education"

202 challenged for containing materal considered "anti-family"[27]

harmful to children but lawful for adult examination, and a substantial quantity of text and pictures harmful to no one.... There is no good reason, then, to treat blocking of adult enquiry as anything different from the censorship it presumptively is.[28]

Ashcroft v. American Civil Liberties Union (2001)/Child Online Protection Act (1998). COPA followed from the Communications Decency Act and was similarly

A wish to protect kids from objectionable material on the Internet led to numerous laws and court cases.

challenged. It worked its way through the court system until reaching the Supreme Court in 2001 after U.S. Attorney General John Ashcroft brought suit against the American Civil Liberties Union (ACLU). COPA said that anyone who made available to minors material that was harmful to them could be fined or imprisoned. Many librarians objected to COPA, as it prohibited them from offering Internet access in their libraries. In her arguments on behalf of the ACLU, attorney Ann Beeson pointed out that many people would censor themselves, which violated their First Amendment rights. She also noted the objection on the part of the libraries, saying that filters to protect minors from adult content were expensiveand had been shown to turn away potential patrons. She argued that "the vast majority of rational speakers, when faced with this choice, are going to self-censor, and that is speech that adults had the right to get."[29] The Supreme Court ruled in June 2004 that COPA was not constitutional. Writing for the majority opinion of the Court, Justice Kennedy said, "Content-based prohibitions, enforced by severe criminal penalties, have the constant potential to be a repressive force in the lives and thoughts of a free people."[30] The Supreme Court also ruled that the lower court had not ruled on all the parts of the case that were in its jurisdiction. The Supreme Court then sent the case back to the lower court for fuller examination of the effectiveness of Internet filters.

In March 2007, Senior Judge Lowell A. Reed, Jr., of the Federal District Court in Philadelphia, struck down COPA. Judge Reed wrote in his decision, "Perhaps we do the minors of this country harm if First Amendment protections, which they will with age inherit fully, are chipped away in the name of their protection."[31] One area of concern for people against the law was that in order to "prove" that an online user was over the age of eighteen, he or she had to provide a credit card number. This could discriminate against people of lower income who do not have credit cards. It also adds another concern to those who are afraid to use credit cards on the Internet.

Using credit cards is not a perfect solution, but other Web sites merely *ask* the user if he or she is at least eighteen. For example, the Web site of Parents Against Bad Books in Schools (PABBIS) says:

> Since some of the material in these K-12 school books is extremely controversial and many people would consider it objectionable or inappropriate for children, we have set up an adult content website for the book material. You will have to verify that you are 18 years of age to enter.... Please click here to access this site.[32]

When admitted to the PABBIS site, the user then has access to all the offensive parts of the books, but not within the context of the book itself. The organization has retyped the content into a list of isolated statements that they find offensive.

Immediately speaking out against Judge Reed's ruling were two analysts for Focus on the Family Action (FOFA), a related but separate group from Focus on the Family. "Should Congress abandon its 'compelling interest' in this area merely because parents have some responsibility there as well?" asked Bruce Hausknecht, a judicial analyst for FOFA.[33]

The second analyst, Daniel Weiss, cited a study by the University of New Hampshire that was recently published in the *Journal of Pediatrics*. According to that study, 42 percent of children had been exposed to pornography online in just the past year. "Kids are getting exposed at alarming rates and harmed by this material," said Weiss. "I think this judge is starting to make clear no law is going to be good enough for these courts."[34]

Chapter 3

Sides in the Battle

In the battle over book banning, the two sides are represented by a number of different groups. These organizations have some differences in focus, agenda, and membership, but they share some common beliefs.

Groups Against Banning

In discussions of challenged books, some groups speak up against banning *any* book. Examples of these are the American Library Association, the National Council of Teachers of English, the American Civil Liberties Union, and the International Reading Association.

- The American Library Association (ALA) was founded in Philadelphia in 1876 "to provide leadership for the development, promotion, and improvement of library and information services and the profession of librarianship in order to enhance learning and ensure access to information for all."[1]

- The National Council of Teachers of English (NCTE) was founded in 1911 "to advance teaching, research, and student achievement in English language arts at all scholastic levels."[2]

- The American Civil Liberties Union was founded in 1920 with the goal of preserving Americans' rights that were granted under the U.S. Constitution. They are especially concerned with people whose rights are often denied. According to the organization's Web site, "If the rights of society's most vulnerable members are denied, everybody's rights are imperiled."[3]

- The International Reading Association (IRA) was established in 1956 for professionals involved in teaching reading.

Joint Statement on Book Banning

The NCTE and the IRA together developed a statement about the banning of books:

> All students in public school classrooms have the right to materials and educational experiences that promote open inquiry, critical thinking, diversity in thought and expression, and respect for others. Denial or restriction of this right is an infringement of intellectual freedom.[4]

In addition to the statement, the NCTE created a CD-ROM with more than 200 defenses of

Terms Related to Book Censorship

ban—To remove or deny access to a book or other material.

censor—To prevent the publication or dissemination of material that is considered objectionable, sensitive, or harmful.

censorship—The act of controlling information or the expression of ideas.

challenge—To file a formal protest against the inclusion of a book in a library or school curriculum.

restrict—To limit the circulation of a book to people of a particular age or those who have parental approval.

more than 170 books. At first, the defenses were sent out individually in response to specific challenges and requests from teachers. The number of requests became overwhelming. The NCTE's Standing Committee Against Censorship and a group called "Support for the Learning and Teaching of English" (SLATE) raised money to make the defenses available on a wide basis. So the CD was created. Volume 2 was released in 2005 with 100 more defenses.

Each defense, called a "rationale," provides an overview of the book's plot as well as the value for students in studying it and a teacher's assigning it. Possible objections are described, along with answers to those objections and alternative books that might be assigned. That way, the teacher can choose another book that addresses similar concepts but is not as offensive. For example, William Golding's *Lord of the Flies* has been suggested as an alternative to *The Chocolate War*, since it addresses some of the same themes but does not have the sexual content.

The rationales can help teachers decide whether the book fits the curriculum and how best to present it. The rationales do more than give librarians and teachers "ammunition" in defending their choices. They also help allay the fears of parents and help administrators make informed decisions when a book is challenged. Some of the rationales were developed by graduate students in their doctoral children's literature classes. Some of the rationales had been published in newspapers and magazines and were gathered by the NCTE.

The NCTE shares one concern in offering the CD: that if teachers know about the possible objections to a book, they might be more inclined to avoid the controversy.

> One might be tempted to pull back and decline to teach a work that is genuinely suitable to the English program and student population. This chilling effect is the opposite of what is intended. The rationales are offered in support of the teacher's best reflections and strongest instincts about program choices. The result of working with these materials should not be a collapse of the will and self-censorship, but rather deepened conviction and heightened professionalism.[5]

Cormier's books on the CD are *After the First Death*, *Beyond the Chocolate War*, *The Bumblebee Flies Anyway*, *The Chocolate War* (two rationales), *Tunes for Bears to Dance To*, and *We All Fall Down*.

Groups Supporting Banning

Certain groups can be counted on to advise caution in exposing young readers to questionable material and often support *removing* books from schools and libraries. Examples of these groups are Focus on the Family, Citizens for Community Values, Parents Against Bad Books in Schools, and Citizens for Literary Standards in Schools.

According to the NCTE and IRA: "All students in public school classrooms have the right to materials ... that promote open inquiry, critical thinking, diversity in thought and expression, and respect for others."

- James Dobson is the driving force behind Focus onthe Family, which he founded in 1977. The non-profit organization's mission is

> to cooperate with the Holy Spirit in sharing the Gospel of Jesus Christ with as many people as possible by nurturing and defending the God-ordained institution of the family and promoting biblical truths worldwide.[6]

- Citizens for Community Values (CCV) is a national organization that was formed in Cincinnati, Ohio, in 1983. According to their Web site, they believe

    that sexually oriented businesses, pornography, obscenity, promiscuity, and sexual abuse threaten the moral fabric of our society. The well being of our communities, the strength of our families, and the hearts, minds, and lives of our children are at risk when traditional values and high community standards are abandoned.[7]

- Parents Against Bad Books in Schools was formed in 2001 in Fairfax, Virginia, to protest a specific book. The organization posts descriptions of "bad" books on its Web site, including quoting and counting

Types of Offensive Language

cursing—Originally meant language that called for great harm, evil, or injury to come to someone, but is frequently used interchangeably now with "swearing."

defamation—Language that injures or destroys the reputation of someone, including libel (which is usually in writing) or slander (which is usually spoken).

obscenity—Language that people find to be repulsive, disgusting, or shocking to their sense of what is moral or decent.

profanity—Language that treats something sacred or holy with great disrespect.

racial or ethnic slurs—Language that expresses hatred or a belief that certain people are inferior to others based on their race or ethnicity.

swearing—Originally meant to make a promise or take an oath, calling upon God to show one's sincerity, frequently used now to describe bad or vulgar language or language that involves divine punishment (such as "damn" or "hell").

each occurrence of an offensive word. According to the PABBIS Web site:

> Bad is not for us to determine. Bad is what you determine is bad. Bad is what you think is bad for your child. What each parent considers bad varies and depends on their unique situation, family and values. The main purpose of this webpage is to identify some books that might be considered bad and why someone might consider them bad. Another purpose of this webpage is to provide information related to bad books in schools.[8]

- Citizens for Literary Standards in Schools is an organization that was formed in 2004 in reaction against books required in the curriculum of the Blue Valley School System of Kansas City, Kansas. Their goal is to

> encourage the public schools to help our children develop a *love of reading* and gain a *rigorous literary education* through excellent literature choices. Sadly, most parents have no idea that *deviant sex including bestiality and pedophilia*, for example, is included in graded reading assignments in their public schools. Rather, schools HIDE adult content from parents and patrons [emphasis in original].[9]

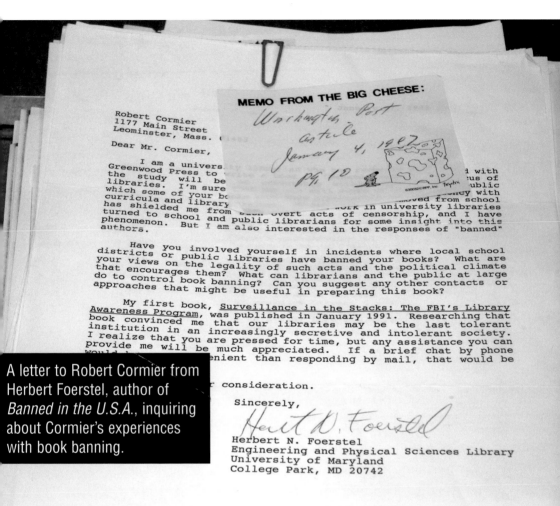

A letter to Robert Cormier from Herbert Foerstel, author of *Banned in the U.S.A.*, inquiring about Cormier's experiences with book banning.

Evidence of Challenges

One of the most thorough resources about book banning is Herbert N. Foerstel's *Banned in the U.S.A.: A Reference Guide to Book Censorship in Schools and Public Libraries*. In the preface to the revised edition, Foerstel writes:

The most obvious conclusion to be drawn ...
is that book censorship in the United States
continues apace. The older conservative
organizations continue to seek out hints of
vulgarity and mysticism in books for children
and young adults, but liberal groups have also
attempted to ban books containing violence
and racial epithets. This emerging censorship
combination bodes ill for free expression.[10]

In 2006, the latest year for which statistics are
currently available, the American Library Association
and other similar organizations received 546 formal
challenges in the form of written complaints filed with
a library or school requesting that materials be removed
because of content.[11] Most of the challenges were not
successful.

As mentioned earlier, the three top reasons that
books are challenged in general are offensive language,
sexuality, and violence. These reasons are echoed in the
challenges against the books of Robert Cormier, especially *The Chocolate War*—the book most often
challenged in 1998 and 2004.[12] Cormier's works have
met with objections mostly on the basis of these reasons, plus his unhappy endings. In Cormier's books,
the characters do not always live happily ever after.
Many of the characters do not live at all.

Chapter 4

Robert Cormier: Asker of "What If?"

Robert Edmund Cormier was born to Lucien Joseph Cormier and Irma Collins Cormier on January 17, 1925. Known as "Bob," he grew up in a neighborhood called "French Hill," in Leominster, Massachusetts. Leominster is about an hour northwest of Boston and halfway between Worcester and the New Hampshire border. Leominster was named after Leominster, England, and is in Worcester County. It was once a manufacturing center for plastic products such as combs; it was known at one time as the "plastic pioneer of the world."[1] (Many descriptions of the comb factory show up in Cormier's books.) The three-story, narrow apartment houses of Leominster also appear often. These "three-deckers," as Cormier called them, were separated by narrow alleys. Many had small porches or balconies that people could sit out on. The residents called them "piazzas," the Italian word for "public

STOR

Robert Cormier, hailed as one of the finest authors of young adult fiction, is also one of the most often challenged.

square," and indeed they were. They helped develop a tight sense of community.

Cormier later described his hometown in the very last book published before his death, *Portrait of a Parish*:

> There were no spires reaching toward the sky when the first Canadians reached Leominster. In 1870, there were only ten families here.... Many others soon followed, however.... A great number of Canadians found their way to Leominster, to the east side of the town where new houses, most of them three-deckers, were

56

being erected on numbered streets to provide living places for the newcomers.

Many of them moved in with relatives and friends, crowding into the five- and six-room tenements until they earned enough to become independent.

The district on the east side quickly became known as French Hill, although not really a hill. Perhaps it was given its name because of the slight inclination of the land as it sloped east of the Boston & Maine railroad tracks....

In the center of Leominster, the town hall, the police and fire stations and the various stores were focused on Monument Square. Beyond, to the west, were the homes of the Yankee families who founded Leominster back in Indian days and forged a bustling, growing town eager to meet the challenges of a new century.

Thus was the stage set in the waning years of the 19th century for the French-Canadians to step forward and realize their dream of a parish to call their own.[2]

In this town, made up primarily of Catholic French-Canadian and Irish immigrants, Lucien and

Irma Cormier raised their family of eight children (from oldest to youngest): Norman, Robert, Leo, Gloria, John, Anne, and twins Constance and Charles. Leo died in 1930 when he was three and Bob was five. Cormier remarked as an adult that he didn't remember much about his brother's death, but he remembered being sent to tell other relatives the bad news.[3]

Cormier's Early Life

When Robert Cormier was a boy, he was allowed to attend movie showings at the local theater on one condition: he had to tell his mother the story as soon as he got home. Cormier pointed out later in life that these sessions with his mother taught him how to tell a story and keep an audience captivated. It was also a tradition that he would pass on to his own children.

Cormier attended mostly Catholic schools during his youth. When he was in seventh grade at St. Cecilia's, one nun in particular encouraged him to write. He later dedicated *Tenderness* to her and two other teachers, saying:

> In memory of the teachers who changed the course of my life
>
> Sister Catherine
>
> E. Lillian Ricker
>
> Florence D. Conlon

Bob had a best friend, Pete, who lived for a while in the same three-decker that Bob did. After a

childhood of being best buddies, though, their friendship began to splinter. Pete broke his leg when they were in sixth grade and missed a lot of school. Bob moved up with his class and Pete fell back a grade. Their drifting apart continued when their apartment house burned down. Bob looked up from his school desk one day when he was in eighth grade to see flames coming from his house and streaking the sky. Knowing that his family was inside, Bob tried to leave. His teacher, a nun, held him back to say his prayers first before she would let him go to try to save his mother and baby sister. As a result of this one nun's actions, Bob began to question his church, but not necessarily his faith. The family survived the fire fine, but the apartment building was destroyed. Because their family homes had been destroyed in the fire, Pete and Bob were placed in the homes of relatives and they saw each other even less.[4]

World War II was under way when Cormier graduated from high school. Cormier was turned down for the armed services because of his nearsightedness. He tried to enlist two more times but was again rejected.[5]

Becoming a Writer

Cormier enrolled in Fitchburg State College, less than five miles away from Leominster. Fitchburg State became an important part of Cormier's life and legacy. When Cormier was nineteen, a teacher of his named Florence Conlon secretly entered one of his essays in a contest. "The Little Things That Count" won $75 and

59

was published. Cormier was on a path to become a great writer.

In 1946, he started working for WTAG, a radio station in nearby Worcester. The "TAG" in the station's call sign stood for "Telegram and Gazette," which was also a newspaper in Worcester. Two years after his start at the radio station, Cormier began working at the paper as a reporter. He wrote a weekly human-interest column, "A Story from the Country," for that newspaper. The same year, Cormier married Constance Senay, known as Connie. He was twenty-three.

A Family Man

Connie and Bob Cormier had four children: Roberta ("Bobbie") in 1951, Peter in 1953, Christine in 1957, and Renée in 1967. Cormier often credited his children with inspiring his stories, and he dedicated many of his books to individual or collective family members and friends. Starting in 1955, Cormier worked as a journalist at the local paper, the *Fitchburg Sentinel and Enterprise*, for twenty-three years.

Although as an adult he loved to travel, Robert Cormier never moved more than three miles away from his birthplace. Readers of Cormier's books will recognize many of the stories' fictional hometowns in Robert Cormier's childhood hometown. The French Hill of his youth became the "Frenchtown" of his works. Leominster became "Monument," and appears (almost as a character itself) in such books as *The Chocolate War*, *Beyond the Chocolate War*, *Heroes*, *Fade*, *After the First*

Death, Other Bells for Us to Ring, Tenderness, and *The Bumblebee Flies Anyway.*

When Cormier was young, a boy was murdered in town. This incident showed up later in *Frenchtown Summer.* Cormier describes his fictional towns as bleak, grey, and predictable—to a point. The same could be said about Cormier's writing itself, as in the following examples. The first is from *Heroes*; the second is from *The Chocolate War:*

> Often, in the evening, when families gathered on the piazzas, the men drinking beer they had brewed in big crocks in the dirt-floored cellars and the women mending socks and knitting as they chatted, I'd seek out Marie.... Although we were separated by that chasm of being twelve years old, when boys and girls barely acknowledged each other's existence, Marie and I spoke to each other once in a while because we lived in the same three-decker. Sitting on the steps, we'd talk about everything and nothing.[6]

> Was this all there was to life, after all? You finished school, found an occupation, got married, became a father, watched your wife die, and then lived through days and nights that seemed to have no sunrises, no dawns and no dusks, nothing but a gray drabness.[7]

61

Images of the Author

Cormier's family and close friends recognized the author in many of his characters. "The boy being chased by dogs, riding bikes, going to the library, scurrying down alleys, [being] part of a large family, playing ball, working in a store, falling in love …," Bobbie Cormier Sullivan, Cormier's oldest daughter, cites as examples.

"My dad was always available to us as we were growing up and as adults," Sullivan says. "Even though he was reading or writing he never shut us out of his writing room, a small alcove off the dining room." She says that her father would get home early after putting the paper to bed. He would then listen to the children's accounts of their day, start supper, and wait for his wife, Connie, to get home from work.[8]

Cormier's youngest daughter, Renée, remembers him as a terrific father. "He always made time for us, even in the midst of his writing," she says. "He was a wonderful listener, very encouraging, and a lot of fun. He had a great sense of humor."[9]

Cormier frequently took the children with him to visit his mother and to the library, where they would check out many books, sometimes books that were not being discussed in school.

Bobbie Sullivan said:

> He was funny and loved to tell jokes and kid around. Even though his novels were very serious, I never thought of my dad as a serious

person. I don't mean that in the way that he did not do his job and carry out the responsibilities of a father and husband but in the way that he was lighthearted and had a twinkle in his eye. He did not isolate himself to write and I never remember him telling us to be quiet or go away. We knew Dad was plotting or working on his writing and so I think we respected his space. I know I did.[10]

The Many Sides of the Writer

Cormier originally wrote under the name of John Fitch IV, the founder of the town of Fitchburg. He had asked to be allowed a pen name, or pseudonym, so that his identity would be protected, but also so that his friends' and neighbors' identities would also be shielded. His columns were mostly human-interest stories in which many local residents might have recognized themselves. His column received the national K. R. Thomson Award in 1974 as the best human-interest column written that year. As a result, he was revealed to be Robert Cormier. He was also honored in 1974 by the New England Associated Press Association for having written the best news story under pressure of deadline.

In one of his columns, Cormier wrote:

The Day of the Jackal [is] absolutely first-rate storytelling, that ancient art ... to engage us with the pace that thrills. Such a pace is found in *Jackal* ... so why read the book? Answer:

63

Robert Cormier as a young man. At this time, he worked as a reporter for the *Fitchburg Sentinel and Enterprise.*

You read it because it is completely absorbing and takes its place with what can be called the "unputdownable" books, if there is such a word. There is now.... One could do worse than be a reader of books.[11]

While still writing for the *Sentinel*, Cormier worked on *The Chocolate War*. He said later that he wrote the book in three main chunks: 1969, 1971, and 1974. By day he was a newspaper man, but by night he worked at becoming an author. Finally, in 1978, with the success of *The Chocolate War* under his belt, he left newspaper writing to write books full time.

Robert Cormier's oldest daughter, Bobbie Sullivan, remembers hearing her father at work on his writing when she was young: "He worked all day and when the house was quiet and we had gone to bed, [and] he had insomnia, the typewriter could be heard beneath my bedroom and the tapping was a comfortable sound that lulled me to sleep."[12]

Cormier's widow, Constance Senay Cormier, points out that her husband had a solid work ethic: "He treated writing like a job. He usually got up at the same time each day, had breakfast and went to the typewriter whether he had something to write or not," she says. "He often said that plots came to him at the type-writer."[13] Cormier would work most of the morning and then after lunch visit one of the three or four libraries in the area. Bob Foley, the director of the library at Fitchburg State College, said that after

Cormier's papers were donated to the college library, he was a frequent visitor there, as well.[14]

In addition to the *Sentinel*, Cormier also wrote for several magazines, including *McCall's*, the *Saturday Evening Post*, and *St. Anthony Messenger*, a Catholic magazine based in Cincinnati, Ohio.

"My dad was very religious," says Bobbie Sullivan. "He had certain saints he was devoted to and their statues were in a prominent place at home. He even dedicated one of his books to these saints."[15]

If readers know Cormier only as the writer of banned books, it might surprise them that Cormier also wrote for *St. Anthony Messenger*, a Catholic magazine. Barbara Beckwith, now the managing editor, recalls working with Cormier. "I remember working with him about his column, which was about his family primarily," she said.[16] (His daughter Renée used to complain that she discovered everything she did ended up in his column, and this was difficult for her when she became a teenager.[17])

Beckwith said:

> He was easy to work with on the column. His prose was precise and elegant. He had a gentle take on life, was a keen observer of the human condition, and that included himself. I think what he wrote for us was different from his newspaper work, and even his novels, because it was personal and reflective."[18]

Epigraphs

English teachers often say that to be a good writer, one must be a good reader. Cormier used literary allusions for his book titles and quoted great literature in his epigraphs. (An epigraph is a quote at the front of a book.) Authors often use epigraphs to set the theme for the book by making a connection for the reader between another known work and what he or she is about to read.

Cormier Book	Quotation	Source
Heroes	"Show me a hero and I will write you a tragedy."	F. Scott Fitzgerald, *Notebook E*
Tunes for Bears to Dance To	"Human language is like a cracked kettle/On which we beat out tunes for bears to dance to/When all the time we are longing to move the stars to pity."	Gustave Flaubert, "Madame Bovary" (translated from the French)
Tenderness	"To know the pain of too much tenderness."	Kahlil Gibran, "On Love," *The Prophet*
After the First Death	"After the first death, there is no other."	Dylan Thomas, "A Refusal to Mourn the Death, by Fire, of a Child in London"
The Chocolate War	"Do I dare disturb the universe?"	T. S. Eliot, "The Love Song of J. Alfred Prufrock"

This reflective side was evident in "Look Who's Writing a Letter to Santa Claus," which was published by *St. Anthony Messenger*, in December 1976:

> So, Santa, I address this letter to you, although it occurs to me that I really don't want or need anything new. Just let me keep what I already have…. Let me continue to cry at sad movies and be delighted by the corny ones, and let the good guys win at the end, once in a while…. And please, dear Santa, let the years deal gently with all the people I love."[19]

Cormier had a special relationship with people, especially teenagers—including his own. "He listened to us and gave good advice when we were young and also later in life," says daughter Bobbie Sullivan. "I particularly enjoyed calling him after seeing a really good movie. He loved the movies and so did I; possibly we all got our love of the movies from him."[20]

"He could talk to anybody without sounding condescending," says Robert Foley.[21]

At one point in *I Am the Cheese*, the main character (Adam) stops at a phone booth to call his friend, Amy. Cormier used his own phone number for Amy's number. When it became widely known that he had done this, teens began dialing the number just to talk to Robert Cormier. Some went along with the novel, pretending they were talking to Amy's father. Some would pretend to be Amy herself. Others called as themselves, just wanting to see if the author would really pick up the phone. Cormier would respond to the callers however they presented themselves. If the callers said they were Adam or Amy, he was Amy's father. If they were themselves, he was Robert Cormier, famous author, being himself.

"Bob was extremely gentle, loving, and caring," says his widow, Constance Cormier. "He was fun, lighthearted, optimistic with a lovely disposition. He saw the best in everyone and was extremely generous with his time with people who called him asking for his advice about how to get started writing."[22]

Miami University associate professor Margaret Sacco saw this as well. "For example, a woman in the UK was writing a thesis on him as a controversial author and she contacted me for research materials and asked me how to contact him," she says. "Cormier picked her up at the airport and gave her an interview to answer her questions and a meal and a ride back to the airport. I do not know too many authors that would do that much."[23]

Cormier's friend, photographer Tony King, noted how people reacted to Cormier. "He was the most authentic man I ever met—unpretentious, and absolutely satisfied with who he was," King says. "Absolute Catholic man, father of children whom he adored, with a wife who was perfect for him."[24]

Sacco said:

Writers must be true to themselves and their readers. I have found the writers that write for young people want to guide young adults through the storms of growing up and becoming adults. There is not any way that any book cannot be controversial. People with dirty minds will always find something. Look at C. S. Lewis, he was considered satanic by some uninformed Christians and he converted more people to Christianity than these ministers that have condemned him and his works."[25]

Besides writing books, Cormier dedicated the last twenty years of his life to his faith, his family, and the fight against censorship. He was frustrated at the challenges to his books but was always willing to add his

Cormier had a special relationship with people, especially teenagers—including his own.

voice to the fray, when possible. He spoke out many times against censorship, frequently banding together with Judy Blume and Nancy Klein, two other well-known authors whose books have often been banned.

Constance Cormier noted that although her husband believed his books should stand by themselves, "he did object to the challenges when he was asked to defend his books … [and] he was always willing to lend his support in censoring battles."[26]

Cormier wrote right up to the end of his life. He died on November 2, 2000. His last work, *The Rag and Bone Shop*, was published in January 2001, a few months after his death.

Daughter Renée Wheeler remembers her father as a wonderful husband to their mother. "Countless people considered him a dear friend," she says. "That's just the way he was. A quiet and giving person."[27]

"He was such a great guy," says Margaret Sacco. "We were friends and I valued his friendship so much.... He was such a marvelous human being.... Our lives have been greatly diminished since his death."[28]

Every year, in November, friends, family members, faculty, and fans gather to pay their respects to Bob Cormier at a reading held in his honor on the campus of Fitchburg State College. Organizer Marilyn McCaffrey includes readings from as many of his works in as many languages as possible. And there are many languages to choose from—French, Spanish, Russian, and Chinese, to name just a few.

Chapter 5

The Chocolate War

The Chocolate War was Robert Cormier's first young adult (YA) book, but it was not his first book. Prior to this work he had published the adult books *Now and at the Hour*, *A Little Raw on Monday Mornings*, and *Take Me Where the Good Times Are*. *Now and at the Hour* was about the death of his father.

Cormier originally wrote *The Chocolate War* without considering a specific audience. He submitted it to seven publishers who rejected it. Fabio Coen, an editor at Pantheon, the eighth publisher to see the manuscript, accepted it but suggested to Cormier that it should be for young adults. Coen also suggested taking out one chapter toward the end. After careful consideration, Cormier agreed with the suggestions and removed the chapter. It was the beginning of a long, respect-filled relationship that produced many books, most of them for young adults.

Cormier's own son, Peter, was the spark behind the creation of *The Chocolate War*. Peter came home one day with news of a candy sale at school. Although it seemed to be for a good cause, Peter asked if the school could force him to sell the chocolates. Cormier encouraged Peter to not sell the chocolates if he did not want to. Peter decided not to, and nothing more came of it. But then Cormier wondered what else might have happened. This "what if?" curiosity shaped many of his books.

What if a boy refused to sell the candy? What if, instead of just being disappointed, the school's leaders took the refusal personally? What if the school was really run not by the administration but by a bunch of bullies? What if …? and a book was born. Cormier took fears that many teenagers feel and gave them a voice. And that is part of what caused the controversy around his writing.

Plot Summary

In *The Chocolate War*, the main character, Jerry, is a new student at Trinity, an all-boys school. His mother has died just before the action of the book starts. Jerry and his father are having trouble in their grief and hardly talk to each other.

Jerry becomes a target of the Vigils, a group of bullies who rule the school. He also earns the wrath of Brother Leon, the teacher who is in charge of the school candy sale, when he refuses to participate. Soon it becomes the top priority of the Vigils' president, Archie Costello, to put Jerry in his place. This is the same mission of the corrupt Brother Leon, who even enlists the help of the Vigils to achieve his goal. Jerry buckles under to the Vigils at first but then ends up making a stand for himself.

The climax of the book occurs when the Vigils arrange a brutal fight between Jerry and one of the biggest bullies in the school. They sell tickets to make money, they encourage people to attend the fight—and then they determine its outcome. Jerry is in the process

Cormier's own son, Peter, was the spark behind the creation of The Chocolate War *when he came home one day with news of a candy sale at school.*

of getting his lights knocked out when the lights in the school stadium actually do go out. The book ends with the wailing of sirens as the ambulance takes him away.

The book is not really about chocolates, or even about school. It is a story about power: who has it, why they have it, and how they use it. Over the course of the book, Jerry becomes a friend, a loner, a hero, and a victim. At the end, however, he does not win. And that bothers many readers.

Literary Devices
Cormier employs a variety of literary devices in The Chocolate War.

Allusion. An allusion is an indirect reference, usually to another piece of literature. Jerry wonders, as the poster in his locker says, "Do I dare disturb the universe?" This line is an allusion to a famous poem by T. S. Eliot, called "The Love Song of J. Alfred Prufrock." The full line reads as follows:

> *Do I dare*
> *Disturb the universe?*
> *In a minute there is time*
> *For decisions and revisions which a minute will*
> *reverse.*

The poem parallels the dilemma facing Cormier's character. The end of the poem reflects a sense of failure for not taking courageous action. Those who know the poem will appreciate the reference to a work that talks about spiritual doubts. Those readers who don't know the poem, however, will still understand the statement's superficial meaning for Jerry, as he questions whether he should disturb his own universe at Trinity High School. Cormier enriches his writing with frequent literary allusions such as this.

Simile and Metaphor. Another literary technique that Cormier used in a lot of his writing was figurative language, especially similes and metaphors. A simile is a direct comparison between unrelated things, using "like" or "as." For instance, Cormier says that the tickets to the fight were selling like dirty pictures. This comparison is unusual, but it helps capture the feeling of misbehavior, fear of being caught, and popularity of the tickets. A page later, he switches similes and says that the tickets were selling "like there was no tomorrow." In this second (common) simile, the reader understands the veiled threat of impending doom— that perhaps there *will* be no tomorrow for Jerry.

A metaphor is like a simile, except that things are compared without the use of "like" or "as." Here is an example of Cormier's use of metaphors, describing Obie, Archie Costello's sidekick:

> Pretend you're a spotlight, Obie told himself, a spotlight sweeping the place, stopping here and there, lingering at other places, picking up the highlights at other places, this momentous occasion.... Obie, the spotlight, concentrated on Renault.[1]

Imagery. Writers of books without illustrations must choose their words so that a reader can picture the action and feel like a participant. Cormier used vivid imagery in describing his characters and situations. For example, Brother Leon, the bully of a teacher, decides to pick on one bookish boy named Bailey:

> "Bailey," Brother Leon said. "Why do you find it necessary to cheat?"

> They say that the hydrogen bomb makes no noise: there's only a blinding white flash that strikes cities dead. The noise comes after the flash, after the silence. That's the kind of silence that blazed in the classroom now."

The Chocolate War has been translated into many languages and is popular with young people all over the world.

Point of View. "Point of view" refers to the perspective from which a book is told. *First person* means that the reader is "in" the head of the main character; the narrative uses "I" and "me" in referring to the narrator. Stories using the *third person* point of view tell the story as if an outsider were narrating it. In third person, the narrator is not a character in the book. When an author uses a *rotating* point of view, he or she tells the story by following many characters. In the following exchange, Cormier demonstrates his use of a rotating point of view. In the earlier example describing metaphors, the point of view was Obie's. In this scene, the reader is following the action from David Caroni's perspective but is not "inside" Caroni's head.

> "On the other hand, Caroni, perhaps the *F* will stand," Brother Leon said. "It depends ..."

> "I see, Brother Leon," Caroni said.

> And he did see—that life was rotten, that there were no heroes, really, and that you couldn't trust anybody, not even yourself.[3]

Cormier rotates point of view well. The reader can feel a connection with all the characters. Therefore, it comes as a surprise when the reader realizes just three pages before the end of *The Chocolate War* that two major characters in the book have not interacted with each other. We—the readers—are familiar with both of the characters. In this section, Jerry's best friend, Goober, is struggling toward Jerry after the fight to help him; he has to fight his way against the current of all the other boys running past him.

> Goober had struggled toward the ring in the darkness and had finally reached Jerry as the lights went on. "We better get a doctor," he had yelled at the kid called Obie, Archie's stooge.
>
> Obie had nodded, his face pale and ghost-like in the floodlights.[4]

Although the readers know who Obie is and have been following him throughout the story, Goober and Obie had never interacted so Cormier identifies him as Goober would think of him: a kid he barely knows as Archie's "stooge."

Theme. Another literary technique is the use of themes, which are ideas that appear and reappear like a thread woven throughout the story. In reading literature, people sometimes discover themes that the author was not aware of when he or she wrote the book. Readers bring their experiences to the book, which then affect how they interpret it.

One of the themes in *The Chocolate War* is the idea of disturbing the universe, introduced by the T. S. Eliot poem. Jerry's universe is disturbed by the death of his mother before the action of the book starts. The poster in his locker with the phrase "Do I dare disturb the universe?" suggests a conscious act. Jerry does, indeed, disturb the universe. So the answer to the immediate question is yes, he did dare. But the next question might be "Was it worth it?"

Objections to the Book

The depressing ending of *The Chocolate War* is one of the reasons that people have objected to the book. Some people also feel that the book shows kids that authority cannot always be trusted. *The Chocolate War* also contains violence, offensive language, frequent references to masturbation, and occasional references to girls' breasts. Aside from these issues, some more subtle concepts are also objected to. For example, the good guys do not always win. Sometimes the bad guys win. (Even in the sequel, *Beyond the Chocolate War*, the good guys *still* do not win.)

The publication *Hit List* noted:

> *The Chocolate War* . . . has been praised by reviewers and critics for its realism, literary style, and its underlying assumption that young adult readers are capable of critical thinking and able to form reasoned opinions about the world they inhabit. Cormier has been lauded for his use of language and symbolism. *The New York Times* has placed this novel on a par with Golding's *Lord of the Flies* and Knowles' *A Separate Peace*. Part of the

novel's appeal to teen readers is its brutally honest picture of school life."[5]

Challenges

The Chocolate War was the fourth most challenged book of the 1990s and was *the* most-challenged book of 1998 and 2004. It is challenged on the basis of language, violence, sexual acts (mostly masturbation), degrading

The themes of *The Chocolate War*, like those of Cormier's other books, are meaningful to many young adults.

references to girls' bodies, its upsetting ending, and a perceived lack of respect for organized religion, specifically Roman Catholicism.

Specific challenges include the following:

- In 1996, *The Chocolate War* was removed from junior high school libraries in Riverside, California. A school district committee ruled that the book was too disturbing to be read by young people without being able to participate in a teacher-led discussion in class.

- In 1997, *The Chocolate War* was removed from the curriculum in three Texas school districts. That means that it could not be used in the classroom by the teacher.[6]

- In 1997, the Broken Arrow board of education in Oklahoma voted to remove the book from the school libraries, even though it had been there for more than twenty years.

- In 1998, *The Chocolate War* was removed from the Greenville (Texas) Intermediate School library for its bad language, blasphemy, and sexual references.

- In 1999, the same reasons were cited in parental requests to remove the book from classrooms in Colton, New York, and South Park, Colorado.

- In 2000, the year that Cormier died, a challenge hit close to home—literally. Parents in Lancaster, Massachusetts (which is seven miles from Leominster) asked that *The Chocolate War* be restricted to juniors and seniors in high school. Robert Cormier got involved in the discussion himself, saying, "I know there are sensitive kids and sensitive parents. My problem is when they want to prevent other people from reading it."[7]

Even though some schools have removed it from the classroom curriculum and the library, *The Chocolate War* is still being used in many school systems.

Chapter 6

I Am the Cheese

Throughout much of *I Am the Cheese*, teenager Adam Farmer is riding his bike to see his family. Or is he? As a young child, he often sang "The Farmer in the Dell" with his father. The last line of that song is "The cheese stands alone." Again, as in *The Chocolate War*, the main character is a boy who stands alone.

Plot Summary

The action of the book shows Adam's long bike ride past bullies and strangers; it is broken up by flashbacks to happier times with his parents. Also shown are flashbacks to what is apparently a series of interviews that are clearly painful for Adam. Even during the memories of happy times with his parents, however, it is clear that all is not well with the Farmers. Adam's parents whisper secrets behind closed doors. Closed doors also hide conversations with a stranger, whose visits seem to bring tension to the home. Evidently, the father

84

is—or was—a journalist and the family is in a witness protection program.

The reader begins to understand that Adam is in some kind of counseling sessions that are being recorded by the therapist. Cormier drops subtle clues that make the reader afraid to trust the therapist. Is he trying to protect Adam, help Adam, or hurt Adam?

> [Adam:] What do you really want to know about me? What's this questioning really about?

> [The therapist:] Must we discuss motive again? We have agreed that these sessions are journeys to discover your past. And I am willing to serve as your guide.

> [Adam:] But I sometimes wonder what's more important—what I find out about myself or what you find out about me.

> [The therapist:] You must avoid these needless doubts—they only delay the process of discovery and you are then left with those terrifying blanks."[1]

By the end of the book, the reader does not know what to believe or whom to trust. And neither does Adam. Cormier tells us this directly, through one of his characters. Early in the book, Adam stops at a gas station to put air in his tires and check a map. A kindly old man in the gas station helps him check his tires and tells Adam, "It's a terrible world out there. Murders and assassinations. Nobody's safe on the streets. And you don't even know who to trust anymore. Do you know who the bad guys are?"[2]

Slowly Adam's "real" circumstances are revealed to the reader, even before they are revealed to Adam. His family had been in a witness protection program, but his parents were killed. Adam has not really been on a bike trip at all. His name is not even Adam Farmer. It's Paul Delmonte. He is in an institution, where he is being interviewed by a counselor. However, the

One of Cormier's readers sent him this fanciful sculpture inspired by *I Am the Cheese*. It is archived with Cormier's literary collection.

counselor is not there to help Adam get better. The pills he is given are not to relieve Adam's headaches or help him remember. The medication is to keep him confused.

The counselor, Brint, is on the same side as Grey, the man who visited Adam's parents. Grey seemed to be in the role of protector, but he is actually the one who had Adam's parents killed. Brint is trying to help Grey by finding out if Adam/Paul can connect Brint with the murder of his parents. Each bit of memory that "Adam" is able to dredge up is another reason for Brint to never let him figure out the truth.

The final, chilling truth is revealed in the last sentence of the book, which quotes a report by Brint on Adam, referred to as "Subject A": "It is advised that (a) … Subject A's confinement be continued until termination procedures are approved or (b) Subject A's condition be sustained until Subject A obliterates."[3]

Literary Devices

In *I Am the Cheese*, Cormier uses many of the writing techniques that he used in *The Chocolate War.*

Allusion. Cormier once again teases the reader with literary allusions that some readers may recognize but others will not. Toward the end of the book, Adam and his parents have gone for a drive to get away from everything. Events have led to the point that the family needs to change location. Adam is wishing that he had said good-bye to Amy Hertz, his one friend.

"Look," his mother said, "let's not talk about all that. This is supposed to be a pleasure trip. A weekend away from Monument. Let's not talk about anything gloomy." … So they drove and his father recited some fragments of Thomas Wolfe, about October and the tumbling leaves of bitter red, or yellow leaves like living light, and Adam was sad again….[4]

Thomas Wolfe's most famous work was a book called *You Can't Go Home Again*—as Adam could not. Another famous Wolfe book is *Look Homeward, Angel*, which is what Adam is trying to do.

Symbolism. When writers use symbolism, they often start with a metaphor or simile. In *I Am the Cheese*, Cormier uses wind as a symbol to represent freedom. As Adam rides his bike, he says (as the narrator), "I let myself join the wind, soaring over the road as I coast beautifully…."[5] Of course, a major metaphor in the book is its title: *I Am the Cheese*. This phrase plays many roles in Cormier's book. It reminds us of an idyllic childhood, where children are sung to and protected by their parents. As the book illustrates and as we find in life, this is not always true. The phrase also reminds us of an accompanying line in the song: "The cheese stands alone." And at the end of the book, Adam/Paul is indeed emotionally alone, although he is surrounded by people.

Imagery. As in his other writing, Cormier makes good use of imagery. When Adam stops at a gas station to check the air in his bike tires, he runs into a "nice old man." Cormier writes, "I want to get away but he's a nice old man, white hair and a face with so many red and blue veins that it resembles the road map in his hands."[6]

Point of View. At first, the reader thinks that *I Am the Cheese* is going to be written as a first-person narrative, where we see the action through the eyes of one character. Then suddenly, the second chapter begins as a translation of a taped interview between two people. It is difficult to tell at first what this transcript has to do with the first chapter about Adam. The second chapter isn't obviously from any one person's point of view, but a tape recorder's. To make matters even more interesting, we begin to suspect that Adam's point of view isn't showing the whole story.

Theme. A classic theme for writers of young adult fiction is "coming of age." In these books, a young man or woman, often a teenager, is trying to establish his or her identity. But by "identity," we usually think of personality or the character's role in his or her world. In this case, Adam truly does not know his identity. Is he Adam, or is he Paul?

As in *The Chocolate War*, another theme in *I Am the Cheese* is that of one individual going up against a large organized group. In *The Chocolate War*, it was Jerry up against the Vigils. In *I Am the Cheese*, that individual on the surface is Adam going against the people who are getting in his way on his bike ride. The individual is also Paul, defending himself against the hounding of the interviewer, Brint. And of course, another individual going against an organization was Adam/Paul's father—and it cost him his life.

Objections

I Am the Cheese has been objected to for its offensive language and violence. More upsetting to some, however, is the role of the government. Once again, authority—in this case, the federal government—is not to be trusted. The government of the book is "protecting" the young boy. (Ironically, in the real world, the government has been asked to intervene to protect young readers from the book.) Some people also objected to *I Am the Cheese* because of its sad ending. In fact, when *I Am the Cheese* was made into a movie in 1983 (starring Robert Wagner as the government psychiatrist), the ending was changed to a happy one.

A Major Challenge

I Am the Cheese was at the root of one of the biggest book censorship battles in the United States in the early 1980s. A group of teachers in Panama City, Florida, tried to make some radical changes to the curriculum in the Mowat Junior High School. Led by the new chairman of the English Department, Ed Deluzain, the teachers tried to replace rote memorization of parts of

A teenager studies in a school library. Throughout history, some have believed that young people need guidance about what they should read.

speech with appreciation of modern literature written specifically for a younger audience. Teachers began to hold book fairs and book swaps. Each classroom had its own mini-library. Students were encouraged to write and even bind their own books.

One of the teachers, Gloria Pipkin, became head of the English Department herself in 1982. In 1985, the

Some people objected to I Am the Cheese *because of its sad ending. When the book was made into a movie, the ending was changed to a happy one.*

National Council of Teachers of English named Mowat a "Center of Excellence" for teaching English.

Pipkin said that during the 1983–1984 school year, her eighth-grade students asked if they could select one of their assigned novels, and two classes chose to read *The Chocolate War*. Many had studied *I Am the Cheese* the year before, and they wanted to read another novel by Cormier.

Because she knew that Cormier's books were frequently challenged, Pipkin discussed the assignment with her principal. She then wrote a letter to tell parents that the class had chosen a book with "strong themes and language."[7] She encouraged parents to read the book, noting that they had the right to request that their children be assigned another book; she also invited them to a meeting at the school to discuss it. One parent came.

A group of parents protested the use of several young adult novels in the district, including those by Cormier. One student's grandmother objected to the use of Cormier's *I Am the Cheese* because of its vulgar language. In response, the superintendent of schools, Leonard Hall, banned the book. Other parents, neighbors, school administrators, and teachers took sides in the debate. The teachers met with the parents and formulated a rule that students had to get their parents' written permission to attend the book fairs or to read any book that was challenged, but this was not acceptable to everyone. One set of parents said that if their daughter (whose grandmother had filed the original complaint) was assigned an alternate book to read, then she would be ostracized—made fun of or avoided.

The debate continued through the late 1980s. A review committee was set up. In 1986 the committee said that *I Am the Cheese* was a "high-interest young adult novel that encourages reading, critical thinking, and class discussion."[8] But Superintendent Hall announced that the book would not be allowed—overruling the recommendation of the committee. He said that he had a petition with nine thousand signatures that supported his decision.

By this time, the story had caught the attention of the news media. A reporter named Cindy Hill decided to do some investigating. She found that the petition said to contain nine thousand signatures really contained only 3,549—and many of those who had signed it were not registered voters in Bay County. Not only did the petition contain the signatures of people who had no right to sign, but even people who did have a right to sign the petition had signed it several times. Some people had signed their children's names as well. Cindy Hill reported this on her evening news broadcast.

Then the critics took the debate out of the gymnasium, classroom, and auditorium. They took it to the streets. Both reporter Cindy Hill and teacher Gloria Pipkin began receiving death threats, along with other teachers. The reporter and teachers took precautions to protect themselves and their families. But the threats did not stop.

On May 12, 1987, forty-four students, teachers, and parents filed a lawsuit in federal court against the superintendent, principal, and Bay County school board. They said that the ban was a violation of their rights under the First Amendment. The first named person on the lawsuit was a student by the name of Jennifer Farrell. As a result, the case is referred to as *Farrell* v. *Hall*, the name of the first plaintiff and the first defendant. In 1988, Judge Roger Vinson said that Hall had been motivated by his own conservative beliefs. He also noted that the school board was within its rights to monitor the literature that was taught in its schools.

By 1991 the battle was over—in Bay County, Florida, at least. The parties involved had agreed to a revised policy for reviewing instructional materials. But in its wake, Superintendent Hall retired, a new school board was elected, and all eleven English teachers had resigned. The NCTE no longer lists Mowat Junior High School's English Department as a "Center of Excellence."[9]

Pipkin wrote ten years later:

> It took five years and a federal law suit to get the banned books restored.... The superintendent and our chief critic marshaled their strongest arguments, including the claim that the book left the reader without hope. Hope is in the heart of the beholder, I told the school board, and the crowds that packed the meeting room. At the end of the novel, when Adam Farmer gets back on his bike once again, I am flooded with hope and inspiration. If a mere child, with incredible institutional odds arrayed against him, can keep pedaling, so can I. So can I."[10]

Chapter 7

After the First Death

After the First Death is a timeless and timely tale of terrorism. The book takes place near a fictitious military base called "Fort Delta." Ben and his parents have transferred there because of a secret spy organization, Inner Delta, which Ben's father is in charge of (although Ben does not know it). The book opens with Ben speaking: "I keep thinking that I have a tunnel in my chest. The path the bullet took, burrowing through the flesh and sinew and whatever muscle the bullet encountered."[1]

Plot Summary

One summer day, a group of four terrorists (three adults and one teenager) hijack a Massachusetts school bus and its load of preschool children. The usual bus driver is not driving this day; his teenage niece has taken his place. Miro is the teenage boy who is working with terrorists Artkin, Antibbe, and Stroll. It is his special assignment to kill the driver of the bus, which will be his first assassination and a sign of his manhood. In the first chapter, he looks forward to killing his first man. But then the driver turns out to be the girl, Kate.

The terrorists have Kate drive the bus to a remote location and stop. The air in the bus gets thick from heat and sweaty children. As the clock ticks, the terrorists make their demands known. They decide to drug the children on the bus. One child is accidentally overdosed and dies.

Finally, the Inner Delta team, which is dealing with the hijacking, makes a decision to try to talk to the terrorists. His father chooses Ben to go in with a decoy message for the hijackers. Ben's father correctly predicts that his son will fold under torture and will reveal the fake information that he has been given. But then the terrorists shoot Ben. The reader then realizes that in all of the father's sections of the book, he is talking to a dead son—a son whose death he indirectly caused. Ben survived the shooting, only to take his own life later:

> I'm sorry, Ben. I was sorry as soon as I told you. As soon as I saw your face and realized what I had done. I thought: I'll make it up to you. If it takes months, years. I'll earn your forgiveness.
>
> *And then I died.*
>
> Oh, Ben.
>
> *Another bridge, another day.*[2]

The reader then realizes that the father has not been looking for Ben at school. As in *I Am the Cheese*, the father has been at a type of hospital or asylum. Ben and his father continue to argue within the father's head, with Ben saying that it is the father's turn to leave; he wants to stay. Their conversation ends with a silence and then Ben saying, "Good-bye, Dad."[3]

Literary Devices

As in his previous books, Cormier utilized a number of literary techniques in *After the First Death*.

Allusion. As with many of his books, Cormier found the title for his work in the vast array of published literature. In this case, Cormier's inspiration was a poem written by Dylan Thomas: "A Refusal to Mourn the Death, by Fire, of a Child in London." The closing lines of the poem read:

> *Deep with the first dead lies London's daughter,...*
>
> *Secret by the unmourning water*
>
> *Of the riding Thames.*
>
> *After the first death, there is no other.*[4]

The last line of the poem is the first line of the book.

There is a connection to another piece of literature as well. William Shakespeare wrote in his play *Julius Caesar,* "Cowards die many times before their deaths;

The valiant never taste of death but once."[5] Common to all three teenagers (Kate, Ben, and Miro) is the desire to prove themselves to someone and to be brave. All three succeed in doing at least that. Two chapters before the end of the book, the reader leaves Kate as she is thinking how alone she is and wondering if she was brave enough during the ordeal: "… and nobody to tell me if I was bra…," she is thinking—when the gun goes off.[6] And *we* are gone. The reader is intimately involved.

Simile and Metaphor. One example also shows Cormier's strong use of similes, as in the following passage. Artkin and Miro have hijacked the bus with all the children on board and Kate at the wheel. Artkin notices that Miro is getting distracted by the children. He reminds Miro that *his* job is to kill the driver.

> He [Artkin] nodded toward the girl. "You have less than fifteen minutes."

> Miro felt the presence of the gun under his jacket, like a tumor growing there.[7]

The character Miro, again, provides an example of a simile. He has just heard the young boy, Ben, deliver the message his father sent him to the terrorists with:

> Miro could not look at [Ben] anymore. As he lowered his eyes, he wondered why he felt such a sense of shame, like a piece of baggage

The Welsh poet Dylan Thomas wrote the line "after the first death...."
Cormier often used lines from great literature in his book titles.

he had not meant to pick up and then found that he could not put down.[8]

Imagery. Cormier's vivid descriptions of the settings help the reader feel the intensity of the situations and the characters in them, even if we don't fully understand what it all means yet. For example, the book has opened with Ben's description of having a hole in his chest. We don't know what he means, but he refers to it again at the end of the first chapter.

> Maybe I should make another and final trip to Brimmler's Bridge before he [his father] arrives.

> And take that sweet plummet into nothingness as the wind whistles through the tunnel in my chest and the hole in my heart.[9]

The hostage children and Kate are forced to stay on the bus with the windows taped shut and the doors locked. Hours pass:

> Night penetrated the bus without Kate being aware of it, the mysterious border between dusk and night dissolved by the darkness. Actually, night only deepened the dimness of the bus, and yet it brought with it a kind of weariness that settled on its occupants like a comforting blanket. The air of the bus was stained with smells: urine (maybe my own,

Kate thought dismally) and sweat and vomit. But somehow they seemed less pungent in the darkness, a trick of the senses maybe.[10]

Point of View. Cormier did an excellent job of portraying the dedication of zealots to their causes: good *and* evil. He makes the reader understand why people might take the actions that they do. One way he does this is by rotating the point of view. Sometimes the reader is inside the mind of teenage terrorist Miro; sometimes we see through the eyes of Kate, the young substitute driver—a teenager herself. We even get into the consciousness and conscience of Ben and his father. As a result, the reader hears the thoughts that the teenage driver is struggling with and how she becomes one of the ultimate heroes of the book. The reader also learns what is driving the teenage terrorist, in particular, who fights for a homeland he has never seen. The reader also hears the thoughts of a man who is paid to be brave and paid to make decisions of national importance as he faces the terrifying personal consequences of those decisions.

The sections from Ben's point of view are written in first-person narrative (as evidenced by the opening sentence, quoted earlier). The father's "scenes" are also in first person. However, the sections from Miro's and Kate's perspectives are in third person. Still, we are able to know what they are thinking, which is a specific form of third-person narrative called "omniscient third."

102

Theme. Over the course of the book, the phrase "the first death" takes on different meanings. Given the title, and the fact that Miro has to kill the driver, the reader immediately begins to think that Kate's murder will be the first death. At first, it seems to refer to the first death that Miro must cause as his rite of passage into adulthood. The first death is—and is not—the death of the bus driver. At other times, it seems to refer to a person's own death, both literal (as in physical death) and figurative (as in emotional death).

> *Cormier does an excellent job of portraying the dedication of zealots to their causes: good and bad. He makes the reader understand why people might take the actions that they do.*

It could refer to the actual first death of a character in the book itself. A young boy is accidentally killed with the drugs that the terrorists use to sedate the children. Readers then later share Kate's horror and anguish as one of her little passengers is killed on purpose. Is this the first death? Cormier even comes out and tells the reader what Miro's first death is, but this is not necessarily the reader's first death: "[Miro] was responsible for Artkin's death. Thus, Artkin had been his first death, not the girl."[11]

Ben's father also imagines Ben's telling him that not only did he *die* twice, but his father *buried* him twice:

"Once in the ground, in the military cemetery of Fort Delta. And again inside of you. Buried me deep inside of you."[12] This explanation is the answer to a question that Cormier asks right at the beginning of the book. Ben is talking "to" the reader and asks, "But how many times is a person allowed to die?"[13] In Ben's case, he is "allowed" to die twice.

Objections

After the First Death contains violence, offensive language, descriptions of bodily functions, and nudity. In addition, like *I Am the Cheese*, it questions decisions made by the government. This time, however, the government is not an intentional villain in the story, as in that book. In *I Am the Cheese*, the government was corrupt. This is not the case in *After the First Death*; people working for the government—especially those led by Ben's father—are just trying to save the hostages. However, *After the First Death* shows that bad things can happen even when the people involved have the best intentions.

With a cute teenage girl as a hostage and a teenage boy as her primary captor, naturally both characters think about bodies and bodily functions. And Cormier actually describes it. In what at first seems to be an attempt at titillation, Cormier gives the girl a weak bladder, causing her to wet her pants several times. However, this character "flaw" makes sense later on in order to put the girl in a situation where the boy accidentally sees her without her pants on. The reactions of both characters enable Cormier to examine topics like gender, power, and society.

Tricia L. Wolfgram Ebner teaches English and reading and is a specialist in teaching gifted students. In her NCTE rationale for teaching *After the First Death*, Ebner suggests that an important discussion that teachers should lead their students in is about "the ethics of using one's own children to attain societal goals." She says that students should also

> discuss and decide whether or not Ben, his father, Kate, and Miro acted in socially responsible manners toward their respective societies.... After students have read this book, they will discuss and think about social actions and the impact of individual actions on an entire society. They will consider current events, such as terrorist and hostage situations, with a little more sympathy for those involved on both sides. In addition, students will try different methods of using plot and point of view in their own creative writing. These changes in student behavior are significant and warrant use of the book.[14]

Ebner's rationale again points out the importance of having such challenging books read with a teacher's guidance. If a book is required as part of a class, a student in that class is under a teacher's direction. However, if a book is just in the library and not required reading, students have no teacher-led discussion to help them understand the book or deal with difficult reactions to it.

Chapter 8

Protecting Kids

"I really sympathize with these people because of their complete sense of righteousness," Robert Cormier said about his fundamentalist critics. "They really believe that they're protecting their children from the world, though that's an impossible thing. That's why they're so hard to fight, because they are so sincere and well-meaning."[1]

Even those who challenged Cormier's books often found him to be a delightful, warm, tough opponent. When Cormier went to Panama City, he spoke for about forty-five minutes to a packed auditorium. He said he wasn't trying to corrupt their children. He told them about his background, about his family and his faith. And they listened—including Charles Collins, the born-again Christian who had led the original complaint with his wife, on behalf of their granddaughter. When Cormier finished speaking, the audience gave him a standing ovation. Afterward, Collins came up to Cormier to shake his hand. Cormier said that Collins told him, "I can't agree with what you write, but I can see where you're coming from. I can admire what you're doing by your own standards."[2] However, not all of those who challenged Cormier's books felt this way.

Challenging Cormier

"*The Chocolate War* met with the most resistance [of Cormier's books]," says Bob Foley, director of the library at Fitchburg State College.[3] Here are just a few recent examples:

- In 1990, it was challenged in Blackwood, New Jersey, because of vulgar language.[4]

- It was also challenged by a minister and his congregation in Landoff, New Hampshire, for "undermining [the] moral fiber of children."[5]

- In 1991, it was challenged in Richmond, Virginia, due to profanity, slang, and sexual allusions.[6]

- A review committee in Greenville, Texas, removed it from the library and from the Accelerated Reader list for fifth and sixth graders in 1998. A former

Mounting a Challenge

There are several ways that parents—or young people—can challenge books:

- Express their concern orally

- Write a letter of complaint to the school or library

- Publicly distribute information challenging the value of the printed material

- Contact an organization such as Family Friendly Libraries/Citizens for Community Values or Parents Against Bad Books[7]

school board member had complained about the book because of blasphemy, bad language, and descriptions of sexual situations. The assistant superintendent said, "This incident is an indication that the system works."[8]

• In 2000, the book was challenged on the eighth-grade reading list of the Lancaster, Massachusetts, school district for language and content. In York County, Virginia, it was challenged for sexually explicit language. The Massachusetts case was the last challenge in which Cormier got personally involved, as he died a few months later.[9]

Rationalizing Objections

In his rationale for *The Chocolate War*, Gary Giannelli wrote:

> At times *The Chocolate War* can be almost too painful to read. It deals with ugly situations and ugly characters. It depicts the hopeless-ness of struggling against injustice. … What, then, is the value of teaching a novel that may, quite fairly, be labeled as a bitter, cynical view of life, that presents awful characters inflicting awful pain on perfect innocents? In fact, it is in its precise, brutally honest miniature por-trait of the world as it is—not as we'd like it to be—that the value and power of *The Chocolate War* lie, especially as a novel for adolescents.[10]

Supporters of Cormier's inclusion of offensive language, including Giannelli, say that Cormier's characters use the same language that many real teens would use in the same life-threatening situations. Author Craig Lancto said:

> The language and sexuality are probably more disconcerting to adults because we would like to think that our thirteen- or fourteen-year-old children never use profanity or think about sex, but Cormier said that his books have credibility with young readers because he uses language and scenes that reflect how kids talk and what they think about."[11]

However, does continuously "pushing the envelope" of good taste define a new standard that the next generation will push? In the same way, if the characters in a book are students who use bad language (even if they do so in private), doesn't that book validate the use of such language by students in real life?

Some argue that the answers to these questions lie in the context in which a book is chosen and taught. An astute teacher can use a discussion of a book's offensive language to address the distinction between civilized behavior and mob rule, for example. However, that assumes that the reader is under the guidance of an astute teacher (or librarian). Some of those who object to the books say that young people who read the books should not do so on their own—that they need the guidance of a teacher or other mentor to put the books

Some people who challenge books say they are only doing what librarians do when they decide whether a book is worth purchasing.

in context for them. This is one of the motivations for concerned adults who have challenged *The Chocolate War*.

In Riverside, California, a "Reconsideration Committee" voted to remove *The Chocolate War* from the middle schools and move all copies of the book to the high school in March 1996. A teacher and a parent objected, arguing that younger middle school students who chose to read the book would not have the oppor-

> *If the characters in a book are students who use bad language, doesn't that book validate the use of such language by students in real life?*

tunity to discuss passages that they found troubling with a teacher.[12]

Similar reasoning was behind the challenges to remove *We All Fall Down* from Carver Middle School in Florida in 2000. In *We All Fall Down*, a family returns to their home to find that vandals have ransacked the house, soiled their belongings, urinated on the walls, and left the fourteen-year-old daughter in a coma. Parents of a sixth-grade girl at Carver complained about the book after she showed it to them, saying "Mommy, this book has cuss words in it." The principal agreed, saying, "We are not going into the book-burning business, but if a book is challenged, we may pull it off the shelves."[13]

We All Fall Down was challenged also in 2000 in the Tamaqua school district in Pennsylvania. The school administrators agreed that they needed a new book-selection policy. "We're walking a fine line here between appropriateness and censorship," said Robert Betz, school board director. "I'm not sure there is an easy answer."[14]

Chapter 9

Book Lovers Fight Back

When Robert Cormier thought of censorship, he did not think of it in general terms of courts or protests. He thought of a specific young girl near his hometown in Massachusetts. Her parents had protested her class's reading *The Chocolate War*. In some schools, when a complaint is filed, the book is immediately removed. In others, the book is still used while a decision is reached, as was the case here. Each day when the class discussed *The Chocolate War*, the girl was sent to the library. One student sent Cormier a letter telling him about the situation and saying he felt sorry for the girl. Ironically, the girl had already read the book on her own the year before and had liked it.

Cormier later wrote in his essay, "A Book Is Not a House: The Human Side of Censorship":

> It struck me then as it strikes me now that in a tender time of blossoming adolescence, when a teenager wants to belong, to be part of the crowd, part of *something*, this girl sat alone in the library, sentenced there by her parents. I wonder which was more harmful—her isolation or reading the novel.[1]

Up until the year that Cormier died, when one of his books was challenged, he often lent his personal support to the teacher or librarian who had chosen it. ReLeah Lent invited Cormier to come to Florida to participate in a series of seminars that they organized with the public library called "A Family Reading Experience," ending with *I Am the Cheese*. Cormier accepted. Lent wrote later:

I couldn't wait to introduce Cormier to these Bay Countians, many of whom had signed petitions against his books, to show them his gentle spirit, his wise and tempered words reflecting an introspective life.[2]

For all the objections to Cormier's work, he has as many defenders. For example, according to author Craig Lancto:

Objections to the violence miss Cormier's point. The contents of the book [*We All Fall Down*] are disturbing but familiar to anyone who reads the newspaper:

Facing a Challenge

Parents—or young people—can counter a challenge by:

• Voicing their concern to the school or library

• Making a written complaint to the school or library

• Attending a school board meeting

• Filling out a Challenge Database form via the American Library Association; contact the National Coalition Against Censorship or the American Booksellers Foundation for Free Expression[3]

vandalism, violence, and victims.... In Cormier's world, actions have consequences that young readers need to see.... Adults who would ban these books want to deny that they reflect the world their children know. That world, familiar to young adults, disturbs the world the adults have constructed in their minds for their children.[4]

"I use Cormier's *The Chocolate War* in teaching," says Miami University's Margaret Sacco. She teaches reading and literacy topics to college students who will then become teachers. "It is considered the best young adult novel of all times by teachers, professors and librarians." Sacco feels that Cormier's books would still have been successful if he had not put anything controversial in them. "However, they would not have been honest," she says.[5]

"He wrote with an incredible amount of integrity and respect for his readers," says daughter Renée Wheeler. "Countless kids identify with his characters and the realism in his stories. He showed that YA books did not always have to have a happy ending."[6]

Honors and Awards

There is no doubt that Cormier's books received a lot of attention. Some of that attention came in the form of prizes and honors from literary organizations.

For example, *The Chocolate War* had plenty of critics, but it had plenty of fans, too. The American

Library Association and *The New York Times* named it, respectively, one of the best books for young adults and best books of the year in 1974. It also won a Lewis Carroll Shelf Award for 1979 and was named to the "Best of the Best 1966–1978" list by the *School Library Journal*. *The Chocolate War* also received the Media and Methods Maxi Award 1976 for best paperback, presented by *Media and Methods Magazine*. The American Library Association named *The Chocolate War* one of the 100 Best Books for Teens from 1966 to 2000.

**Celebrate
the right to read.**

Banned Books Week
September 23-30, 2006

This poster from the American Library Association advertises Banned Books Week. People who object to book challenges say they are upholding the First Amendment.

The Chocolate War, I Am the Cheese, and *After the First Death* established Robert Cormier as a master of the young adult novel. In 1991, the Young Adult Services Division of the American Library Association presented him with the Margaret A. Edwards Award, citing the trio of books as "brilliantly crafted and troubling novels that have achieved the status of classics in young adult literature."[7]

The New York Times called *I Am the Cheese* an Outstanding Book of the Year for 1977. It was also named by the American Library Association as one of the

100 Best Books for Teens from 1966 to 2000, along with *After the First Death*.

After the First Death won several other awards, including an "Outstanding Book of the Year" award from *The New York Times* in 1979. The American Library Association included *After the First Death* many times on its lists of best books for young adults and best books for teens. In 1991, Cormier was the third recipient of the ALA's Margaret A. Edwards Award, which is given to an author whose work touches the hearts and lives of young adults over a period of years. Cormier received the award specifically for his books *After the*

When one of Cormier's books was challenged, he often lent his personal support to the teacher or librarian who had chosen it.

First Death, The Chocolate War, and *I Am the Cheese*.[8] In 1980, *8 Plus 1*, an anthology of short stories that appeared in such publications as *The Saturday Evening Post*, *The Sign*, and *Redbook* was published. In later years, some of the stories in the collection, such as "The Moustache," "President Cleveland, Where Are You?" and "Mine on Thursdays," appeared in anthologies and school textbooks. The collection also received the World of Reading Readers' Choice Award, sponsored by Silver Burdett & Ginn, especially notable because young readers voted for Cormier to receive the prize.

Frenchtown Summer won the *Los Angeles Times* Book Prize for Young Adult Fiction in April 2000. *In the*

117

Middle of the Night and *Tenderness* were nominated for the Carnegie Medal in England, and *Heroes* received a "Highly Commended" citation for that same award. These are unusual honors because the Carnegie Medal is traditionally awarded to a British book.

Photographer Tony King feels that even with all these awards and honors, Cormier was not as appreciated or well known as he might have been. "He was a shadow," says King. "He'd have been as well known as Kurt Vonnegut if he had been writing for adults."[9]

Chapter 10

Beyond the Twentieth Century

Even before his death, Robert Cormier recognized the value in allowing other people access to the materials behind his published works. On May 3, 1981, he donated boxes and boxes of his files to the Fitchburg State College Foundation, to be housed in the Amelia V. Gallucci-Cirio Library. As of 1986, the collection included 131 cartons—84 linear feet of documents— prepared by Fitchburg State's Robert Foley. Foley himself donated some materials as well, including fifty "John Fitch IV" columns, five published short stories, numerous book reviews, various criticism and interpretations of Cormier's work, and some biographical items.[1] The collection also contains mementos that Cormier's fans sent to him, such as a mouse sculpture with a wedge of cheese.

People who have grown up using personal computers might not grasp the hard work that went into typing the many papers that fill the files. Cormier used a manual typewriter, which required striking the keys

This is the library at Fitchburg State College, which houses the files that Cormier donated.

hard. There was no correcting key; there was no "delete" button.

"He had two old manual typewriters," says King. "One was always being fixed and one was being used. Oh, the noise of it!"[2]

The Robert E. Cormier Collection takes up an entire room in the library and is contained on many floor-to-ceiling shelves. Cormier appears to have been a meticulous and organized note-taker. For each book he wrote, he kept a carbon copy or photocopy of the original manuscript reflecting what he had sent to the publishing house. If an editor called and he wrote notes on the manuscript, he filed those, too. If the editor wrote him a letter, he filed the letter. He also filed a copy of his response to the editor. In the current era of e-mails and electronic versions of manuscripts, Cormier's file-keeping practices are a librarian's dream.

An Author's Correspondence
Within these files is Cormier's carbon copy of the cover letter to *The Chocolate War* when he sent it to Fabio Coen at Pantheon.

Leominster, Mass.
June 4, 1973

Mr. Fabio Coen
Pantheon
201 E. 50th Street
New York City

Renée Cormier Wheeler and her daughters at the annual Robert Cormier tribute at Fitchburg State College.

Dear Mr. Coen:

Just a note to tell you how much I enjoyed meeting and talking with you last Friday. I appreciate all your considerations and courtesies and, of course, your interest and suggestions concerning the novel.

I have been pondering our talk and the notes and feel that they can be incorporated into the novel and make it tighter and sharper. At this point, I think it's entirely possible that the changes should all be made by the end of June.

Again, my thanks. It was good of you to spend the time discussing The Chocolate War and I hope that it lives up to your expectations.

With warm personal wishes,

Sincerely yours,
Robert Cormier [3]

Also in the collection is Cormier's letter that accompanied the revised manuscript. Coen had suggested some changes, which Cormier made. (Cormier probably hand-wrote Coen's name in the salutation, where it says "Dear" with nothing after it. This practice was common to show a warm relationship between correspondents.) It is interesting to see Cormier's explanation for why he made some changes and not others:

Leominster, Mass.
June 24, 1973

Mr. Fabio Coen
Pantheon
201 E. 50th Street
New York City
Dear

Enclosed you will find the Chocolate War with the changes that we discussed in our office. I think it's a better novel now—much tighter…

These are the major revisions:

I have eliminated the masturbation chapter. I realize now that this was the weakest chapter in the book as far as contributing to character delineation for forward progress is concerned. True, it led to Archie's choice of Emile Janza as Jerry's antagonist—but the choice was an obvious one to begin with.

The early chapter in which Jerry looks at the girlie magazine in the drug store and then is confronted by the hippie-like character has been drastically reduced. I did not eliminate it altogether because (1) I wanted to portray Jerry instantly as heterosexual. I had just introduced all those boys in a private boys' school and wanted to immediately stress heterosexuality. (2) I retained the hippie encounter, although sharply cut, because this was Jerry's first doubt about his life, where he was going, and, of course, I feel this is essential in his later refusal to sell the chocolates....

The fight scene has been removed from the school auditorium to the athletic field—I am grateful for your suggestion about this because it particularly opened up so many possibilities.... The fight has been shortened and Jerry has been allowed to retaliate against Janza and, yet, his plight is, of course, foreshadowed by the previous events in the novel and he can't possibly win....

The Robert E. Cormier Collection includes more than 130 boxes of materials, including newspaper columns, correspondence, drafts of Cormier's work, and mementos.

... I hope you will excuse the state of the manuscript—I am not the greatest typist in the world and figured that it was essential to get the manuscript to you prior to the end of June rather than waste precious time retyping pages.

I hope you like the changes. If some aren't what was intended, please let me know and we can go over them. My intention at this time is to produce the best novel I can and I, of course, appreciate your help and anything you can do toward that goal....

Sincerely yours,

Robert Cormier [4]

In the exchange between Cormier and Coen, we can also see some of the legal issues in book publishing. The idea that sparked *The Chocolate War* was based on the experience of a real person, Peter Cormier, but other than that, the characters and events in the book were Cormier's invention.

In a letter dated October 26, 1973, Coen addresses this issue in a letter to Cormier:

Dear Bob:

Marilyn reminds me of your wish to dedicate your book to your son Peter. This I had not forgotten and I can assure you it will appear in the book.

As for the disclaimer which you wish to be printed, here is the proposed wording:

THE CHOCOLATE WAR is a work of fiction. All names, characters, and events are fictional, and any resemblance to real persons or actual events is unintentional.

However it is important to remember that if you modeled any of the characters or the school described in the book after real people, or the school near your home, and if they are in fact recognizable as such by others in your neighborhood, we could incur liability and we would have to submit the manuscript to our legal department for a liability and invasion of privacy reading. I would appreciate therefore if you could confirm that the above disclaimer in fact states the truth....

I hope that all goes well with you and would like very much to hear what you are doing and whether the second novel we discussed is progressing.

With my best regards,

> *Sincerely yours,*
> *Fabio Coen[5]*

What's Next?

Fitchburg Library Director Bob Foley has big plans for the Cormier Collection. "There are still more boxes of his material that Connie is donating," he says. "It would take one person working almost full time to do it justice."[6]

Cormier left not only a full collection of life's work for cataloguing, he also left work that still raises issues years after his death. One of Cormier's many obituaries, published in London's *Independent*, noted that Robert Cormier had died "leaving critics with the difficult task of assessing and finally agreeing upon the abiding merits of his contribution to the turbulent world of teenage fiction during the last 30 years."[7]

Cormier broke ground for future writers in the area of young adult literature. His biographer and friend, Patty Campbell, wrote:

> Robert Cormier was, and remains, the consummate master of young adult literary fiction. He was the first to show the literary world that YA novels could be not only realistic about adolescent concerns but also unflinchingly honest about the big questions like the abuse of power, the roles of courage and forgiveness and redemption, and the struggle to stay human in the face of evil.[8]

Cormier's daughter Bobbie Sullivan said:

> He has filled the gap with his books and now young people can read about characters that

have the same lives as themselves. Maybe this leads to self discovery for them, maybe it just lets them know that they are not the first ones to feel the up and down emotions of growing up. The value is he wrote difficult and complex books and kids can understand and define themselves when reading them. Teachers who are teaching these books can lead discussions and pull out themes and morals. Within a classroom setting the books become wonderful teaching tools about life and just growing up."[9]

Cormier is remembered fondly by many outside his family, as well. "I have no right to miss him the way I do, because I didn't know him well enough," photographer Tony King notes wistfully.[10]

"While I still mourn his passing," ReLeah Lent wrote, "his brilliant words, his compassion, and his courage will mean that, at least for me, I will never be the cheese."[11]

Cormier once wrote in a column called "Those Who Don't Make Headlines":

I thought of … how quietly we arrive and depart. And how a man can be born and later die without disturbing the universe, never making headlines and his death announced in eight-point type. I thought of all the men, good men, who are born and who marry and bring children into the world. They work and make love and have good times and

129

bad times and they love their wives and
children without making a fuss about it all
and then they die. I thought of my own father,
who came and went and gave me life. The
earth should stop turning for a while or

Cormier in his study, surrounded
by books and papers.

lightning should split the sky when a good man dies. But nothing happens.[12]

When he wrote this, Cormier was thinking of one man and yet every man. He was thinking of his father, all fathers, and those who would never be fathers. However, the same cannot be said for him. Although the earth did not stop turning and lightning did not split the sky, Robert Cormier's passing was not without notice. He dared to disturb the universe.

1. Are there any topics that you think should *always* be forbidden in books for young people? Why?

2. Are there things (such as books, games, or movies) that you are allowed to see but your friends are not—or vice versa? How does that affect your friendship?

3. Who should decide what goes on the shelves of a school library? What about a public library?

4. Do you think that a community has the right to decide what is allowed in its school or public libraries? If not, who has the right to decide?

5. Are there movies that you are allowed to see or books that you are allowed to read that your parents could not see or read when they were your age?

6. Why do you think Robert Cormier didn't just take out the parts of his books that people objected to?

7. Is there value in the disagreement over book challenges?

387 B.C.E.—Plato suggests banning the *Iliad* and the *Odyssey* because of their potential bad influence on young people.

1450 C.E.—Gutenberg invents the printing press in Germany, making it easier for the average person to read.

1470—First German office of censorship created.

1650—First banning of a publication in the American colonies because it contradicted accepted religious beliefs: *The Meritorious Price of Our Redemption*.

1873—Comstock Act is passed granting the authority to confiscate books thought to be "lewd, indecent, filthy or obscene."

1925—Robert Edmund Cormier is born January 17, 1925.

1933—Nazis burn books in Germany.

1936—Parts of the Comstock Act are declared unconstitutional.

1944—Cormier's story, "The Little Things That Count," is entered by his teacher into a contest. It wins $75 and is published.

1946—Cormier starts at WTAG radio.

1948—Cormier begins writing for the *Worcester Telegram and Gazette*. Cormier marries Constance Senay.

1951—Roberta ("Bobbie") Cormier is born.

1953—Peter Cormier is born.

1955—Cormier begins writing for the *Fitchburg Sentinel and Enterprise*.

1957—Christine Cormier is born; Bob Cormier is promoted to wire editor of the *Sentinel*.

1959—Cormier receives first prize for news writings from the Associated Press in New England.

1960—*Now and at the Hour* (adult) is published by Coward-McCann.

1966—Cormier is promoted to associate editor of the *Sentinel*.

1967—Renée Cormier is born.

1969—Cormier begins writing his column for the *Sentinel* under the pen name of "John Fitch, IV."

1973–74— Cormier receives first prize for news writings from the Associated Press in New England.

1974— Cormier's is named "best newspaper column," Thomson Newspapers, Inc. *The Chocolate War* is published by Pantheon. *The Chocolate War* receives a *New York Times* Outstanding Book of the Year Award and American Library Association Award for books for young adults.

1975—The Island Trees School District in Long Island, New York, removes nine books from the school library because they are "anti-American, anti-Christian, anti-Semitic and just plain filthy." Students, led by Steven Pico, seventeen, sue the school board in the U.S. District Court, claiming their First Amendment rights had been denied. They win.

1977—*I Am the Cheese* is published by Pantheon and is named a *New York Times* Outstanding Book of the Year. Cormier receives an Honorary Doctor of Letters from Fitchburg State College and leaves the *Sentinel* to be a full-time novelist.

1978—Cormier receives the Woodward School Annual Book Award.

1979—*After the First Death* is published by Pantheon. It is named a *New York Times* Outstanding Book of the Year.

1981—The Robert E. Cormier Collection is established within the Fitchburg State College Library.

1991—Cormier wins the Margaret A. Edwards Award for *The Chocolate War, I Am the Cheese,* and *After the First Death. I Have Words to Spend: Confessions of a Small-Town Editor* is published by Delacorte.

2000—Cormier receives the *Los Angeles Times* book award for *Frenchtown Summer. Portrait of a Parish,* Cormier's one-hundred-year celebration of St. Cecilia's Church, is published. Robert Cormier dies in Boston, Massachusetts, on November 2, 2000, from a blood clot following a brief illness.

2001—Cormier's last book, *The Rag and Bone Shop,* is published posthumously by Delacorte.

Chapter Notes

Chapter 1.
Battling Over Chocolate

1. Conversation between the author (who was donating the book) and the librarian at St. Catharine of Siena Elementary School in Cincinnati, Ohio, March 2003.

2. E-mail from Margaret Sacco to author, April 24, 2006.

3. Ibid.

4. "EPA's Top 100 Authors: Cormier, Robert," 1999, <http://www.edupaperback.org/showauth.cfm?authid=80> (April 15, 2006).

5. Random House, Inc., "Robert Cormier: Author Spotlight," n.d., <http://www.randomhouse.com/author/results.pperl?authorid=5740> (April 15, 2006).

6. Telephone conversation between Dr. Marilyn McCaffrey and author, October 27, 2005.

Chapter 2.
Book Banning: A History

1. Lyndon B. Johnson, "Remarks Upon Signing Bill Amending the Library Services Act," February 11, 1964, The American Presidency Project, <http://www.presidency.ucsb.edu/ws/index.php?pid=26067> (May 21, 2007).

2. Claire Mullally, "Libraries & First Amendment: Overview," First Amendment Center, February 9, 2006,

<http://www.firstamendmentcenter.org/speech/libraries/
topic.aspx?topic=banned_books> (April 26, 2006).

3. John Milton, "Aeropagitica," *Bartleby.com*, "Great
Books Online," n.d. <http://www.bartleby.com/3/3/
2.html> (April 26, 2006).

4. Mel Krutz, "Hazelwood: Results and Realities," in
*Preserving Intellectual Freedom: Fighting Censorship in Our
Schools*, Jean E. Brown, ed. (Urbana, Ill.: National Council
of Teachers of English, 1994), p. 216.

5. Claire Mullally, "Libraries & First Amendment:
Overview."

6. "Comstock Law," *Timeline of U.S. History*, n.d.,
<http://shs.westport.k12.ct.us/jwb/AP/TLdocs/comstock.h
tm> (April 26, 2006).

7. Shel Silverstein, *Uncle Shelby's ABZ Book: A Primer for
Tender Young Minds* (New York: Simon & Schuster/Fireside,
1961), no page numbers.

8. American Civil Liberties Union, "Government
Censorship Would Be Harmful," in *Censorship:
Contemporary Issues Companion*, Kate Burns, ed. (New
York: Thomson Gale, 2004), p. 115.

9. "Judy Blume, Carolivia Herron and Cammie
Mannino 'Speaking Freely' Transcript," First Amendment
Center, September 28, 2000, <www.firstamendment
center.org/about.aspx?id=12084> (July 3, 2007).

10. Robert Cormier, untitled essay on censorship,
Robert Cormier Collection at Fitchburg State College,
Amelia V. Gallucci-Cirio Library, Fitchburg, Mass, undated.

11. Syllabus, United States et al. v. American Library Association, Inc., et al., Appeal from the United States Distric Court for the Eastern District of Pennsylvania No. 02–361 (Argued March 5, 2003—Decided June 23, 2003), <http://www.supremecourtus.gov/opinions/ 02pdf/02-361.pdf> (March 18, 2007).

12. Heather Shoenberger and Ben Miller, "Inappropriate Reading?" *Missourian News*, August 21, 2005, <http://www.columbiamissourian.com/news/ story.php?ID=15487> (October 15, 2005).

13. "Film Ratings," The Motion Picture Association of America, 2005, <http://www.mpaa.org/FilmRat ings.asp> (April 26, 2006).

14. Entertainment Software Rating Board, 2006, <http://www.esrb.org/index-js.jsp> (April 26, 2006).

15. Robert Cormier, "Some thoughts on censorship," ms., undated. The Cormier Collection, Fitchburg State College, Fitchburg, Mass.

16. J. M. Coetzee, *Giving Offense: Essays on Censorship* (Chicago: The University of Chicago Press, 1996), pp. vii, 9.

17. E-mail from Tony Greiner to author, June 22, 2006.

18. Herbert N. Foerstel, *Banned in the U.S.A.: A Reference Guide to Book Censorship in Schools and Public Libraries* (Westport, Conn.: Greenwood Press, 2002), p. 79.

19. Ibid., p. 82.

20. "The Most Frequently Challenged Books of 1990–2000," American Library Association, n.d., <www.ala.org/ala/oif/bannedbooksweek/bbwlink/100mostfrequently.htm> (February 8, 2005).

21. Foerstel, p. 83.

22. Ibid., p. 87.

23. The Oyez Project, *Board of Education* v. *Pico*, 457 U.S. 853 (1982), <http://www.oyez.org/oyez/resource/case/1060/> (May 21, 2007).

24. *Board of Education, Island Trees School Union Free School District No. 26 v. Pico*, 457 U.S. 853 (1982).

25. Foerstel, pp. 113–114.

26. Syllabus, United States et al. v. American Library Association, Inc., et al.

27. "Censorship Challenges by Categories, 1990–2000," American Library Association, n.d., <http://www.ala.org/ala/oif/bannedbooksweek/challengedbanned/challengedbanned.htm#hlmcbt> (February 11, 2008).

28. Syllabus, United States et al. v. American Library Association, Inc., et al.

29. The Oyez Project, *Ashcroft* v. *American Civil Liberties Union*, 542 U.S. 656 (2004), Oral Argument, <http://www.oyez.org/cases/2000-2009/2003/2003_03_218/argument> (June 29, 2007).

30. Justice Kennedy, "Opinion of the Court, Supreme Court of the United States, No. 03-218, *John D. Ashcroft, Attorney General, Petitioner, v. American Civil*

Liberties Union et al., On Writ of Certiorari to the United States Court of Appeals for the Third Circuit," June 29, 2004, <http://www.supremecourtus.gov/opinions/03 pdf/03-218.pdf> (March 25, 2007), pp. 5–6.

31. Ian Urbina, "Court Rejects Law Limiting Online Pornography," *New York Times*, March 23, 2007, <http://www.nytimes.com/2007/03/23/us/23porn.html ?_r=1&th&emc=th&oref=slogin> (March 23, 2007).

32. "Welcome!" Parents Against Bad Books in Schools, n.d., <www.PABBIS.com> (April 13, 2007).

33. Wendy Cloyd, "Family Advocates Call COPA Ruling 'Troubling,'" *Focus on the Family CitizenLink.com*, March 22, 2007, <http://citizenlink.org/CLtopstories/ A000004183.cfm> (March 25, 2007).

34. Ibid.

Chapter 3.
Sides in the Battle

1. "Mission, Priority Areas, Goals," American Library Association, 2006, <http://www.ala.org/ala/ ourassociation/governingdocs/policymanual/mission.ht m#mission> (April 13, 2007).

2. "About NCTE," The National Council of Teachers of English, 2007, <http://www.ncte.org/about> (April 13, 2007).

3. "About Us," American Civil Liberties Union, n.d., <http://www.aclu.org/about/index.html> (April 13, 2007).

4. NCTE/IRA, "Introduction," *Rationales for Challenged Books*, NCTE CD-ROM, Version 1.0, NCTE Stock Number: 38276, NCTE, 1998.

5. Ibid.

6. "Our Mission, Vision and Guiding Principles," Focus on the Family, 2006, <http://www.focus onthefamily.com/aboutus/A000000408.cfm> (April 13, 2007).

7. "Mission and Vision: Who Is CCV?" Citizens for Community Values, 2006, <http://www.ccv.org/about us.aspx> (April 13, 2007).

8. "Welcome!" Parents Against Bad Books in Schools, n.d., <www.PABBIS.com> (April 13, 2007).

9. "The Spirit of This Website," Citizens for Literary Standards in Schools, 2004, <www.classKC.org> (April 13, 2007).

10. Herbert N. Foerstel, *Banned in the U.S.A.: A Reference Guide to Book Censorship in Schools and Public Libraries* (Westport Conn.: Greenwood Press, 2002), p. xii.

11. Macey Morales, "'And Tango Makes Three' tops ALA's 2006 list of most challenged books," American Library Association, March 6, 2007, <http://www.ala. org/Template.cfm?Section=presscenter&template=/Con tentManagement/ContentDisplay.cfm&ContentI D=151926> (March 24, 2007).

12. Valerie Strauss, "Bonus Points: Challenges to Books on the Rise," *Washington Post*, October 11, 2005, p. A06.

Chapter 4.
Robert Edmund Cormier: Asker of "What If?"

1. "Combing Through Leominster's History," 2003, <http://www.leominsterbook.com/index.html> (June 24, 2006).

2. Robert Cormier, excerpt from *Portrait of a Parish*, St. Cecilia Church, 2000, <http://stceciliachurch.net/history.htm> (June 24, 2006).

3. Sarah L. Thomson, *Robert Cormier*, The Library of Author Biographies (New York: Rosen, 2003), p. 18.

4. Patty Campbell, *Robert Cormier: Daring to Disturb the Universe* (New York: Delacorte, 2006), p. 19.

5. Campbell, p. 20.

6. Robert Cormier, *Heroes* (New York: Random House, 1998), p. 15.

7. Robert Cormier, *The Chocolate War* (New York: Random House, 1974), p. 64.

8. Letter from Bobbie (Cormier) Sullivan to author, April 2, 2006.

9. Personal letter from Renée (Cormier) Wheeler to author, April 2, 2006.

10. Letter from Bobbie (Cormier) Sullivan to author, April 2, 2006.

11. Robert Cormier, "The Next Best Seller," *I Have Words to Spend: Reflections of a Small-Town Editor*, Constance Senay Cormier, ed. (New York: Bantam Doubleday Dell, 1991). Originally published in the *Fitchburg Sentinel and Enterprise*, August 10, 1971.

12. Letter from Bobbie (Cormier) Sullivan to author, April 2, 2006.

13. Letter from Constance Cormier to author, April 8, 2006.

14. Interview with Robert Foley, November 17, 2005.

15. Letter from Bobbie (Cormier) Sullivan to author, April 2, 2006.

16. E-mail from Barbara Beckwith to author, April 28, 2006.

17. Letter from Renée (Cormier) Wheeler to author, April 28, 2006.

18. E-mail from Barbara Beckwith to author, April 28, 2006.

19 Robert Cormier, "Look Who's Writing a Letter to Santa Claus," *I Have Words to Spend: Reflections of a Small-Town Editor*, Constance Senay Cormier, ed. (New York: Bantam Doubleday Dell, 1991).

20. Letter from Bobbie (Cormier) Sullivan to author, April 2, 2006.

21. Interview with Robert Foley, November 17, 2005.

22. Letter from Constance Cormier to author, April 8, 2006.

23. E-mail from Margaret Sacco to author, April 24, 2006.

24. Telephone interview with B. A. "Tony" King, March 23, 2007.

25. Email from margaret Sacco to author, April 24, 2006.

26. Letter from Constance Cormier to author, April 8, 2006.

27. Letter from Renée (Cormier) Wheeler to author, April 2, 2006.

28. E-mail from Margaret Sacco to author, April 24, 2006.

Chapter 5.
The Chocolate War

1. Robert Cormier, *The Chocolate War* (New York: Random House, 1974), pp. 233–234.

2. Ibid., p. 42.

3. Ibid., p. 115.

4. Ibid., p. 258.

5. Gary Gianelli, "The Chocolate War," in *Rationales for Commonly Challenged Taught Books*, Diane P. Shugert, ed.,special issue, *Connecticut English Journal*, vol. 15, no. 1, 1983. As accessed from the NCTE CD-ROM. Version 1.0, NCTE Stock Number: 38276, NCTE, 1998.

6. "PABBIS Book Excerpts," n.d., <http://www.sibbap.org/bookstheh.htm> (May 18, 2006).

7. Herbert N. Foerstel, *Banned in the U.S.A.: A Reference Guide to Book Censorship in Schools and Public Libraries* (Westport, Conn.: Greenwood Press, 2002), p. 204.

Chapter 6.
I Am the Cheese

1. Robert Cormier, *I Am the Cheese* (New York: Dell Publishing Company, 1977), p. 131.

2. Ibid., p. 24.

3. Ibid., p. 220.

4. Ibid., p. 129.

5. Ibid., p. 15.

6. Ibid., p. 23.

7. ReLeah Lent and Gloria Pipkin, "We Keep Pedaling," *The ALAN Review*, vol. 28, no. 2 (2001), p. 9, <http://scholar.lib.vt.edu/ejournals/ALAN/v28n2/lent.html> (March 22, 2007).

8. Herbert N. Foerstel, *Banned in the U.S.A.: A Reference Guide to Book Censorship in Schools and Public Libraries* (Westport, Conn.: Greenwood Press, 2002), p. 42.

9. Ibid., pp. 43–50.

10. Lent and Pipkin, p. 9.

Chapter 7.
After the First Death

1. Robert Cormier, *After the First Death* (New York: Random House, 1979), p. 3.

2. Ibid., p. 227.

3. Ibid., p. 229.

4. Dylan Thomas, "A Refusal To Mourn The Death, By Fire, Of A Child In London," The Poetry Archive, 2005, <http://www.poetryarchive.org/poetryarchive/singlePoem.do?poemId=7092> (May 5, 2007). Originally published in *Collected Poems of Dylan Thomas* (New York: New Directions).

5. William Shakespeare, *Julius Caesar*, Act II, Scene 2.

6. Cormier, *After the First Death*, p. 221.

7. Ibid., p. 31.

8. Ibid., p. 208.

9. Ibid., p. 15.

10. Ibid., p. 166.

11. Ibid., p. 233.

12. Ibid., p. 227.

13. Ibid., p. 5.

14. Tricia L. Wolfgram Ebner, "After the First Death," in NCTE/IRA, *Rationales for Challenged Books*, NCTE CD-ROM, Version 1.0, NCTE Stock Number: 38276, NCTE, 1998.

Chapter 8.
Protecting Kids

1. Herbert N. Foerstel, *Banned in the U.S.A.: A Reference Guide to Book Censorship in Schools and Public Libraries* (Westport, Conn.: Greenwood Press, 2002), p. 154.

2. Ibid.

3. Interview with Robert Foley, November 17, 2005.

4. Jean E. Brown, ed., *SLATE on Intellectual Freedom* (Urbana, Ill.: National Council of Teachers of English, 1994), p. 14.

5. Ibid., p. 15.

6. Ibid.

7. Joan Vos MacDonald, *J. K. Rowling: Banned, Challenged, and Censored* (Berkeley Heights, N.J.: Enslow Publishers, Inc., 2008), p. 125.

8. Foerstel, p. 202.

9. Ibid., p. 204.

10. Gary Gianelli, "The Chocolate War," in *Rationales for Commonly Challenged Taught Books*, Diane P. Shugert, ed., special issue, *Connecticut English Journal*, vol. 15, no. 1, 1983. As accessed from the NCTE CD-ROM. Version 1.0, NCTE Stock Number: 38276, NCTE, 1998.

11. Craig Lancto, "Banned Books: How Schools Restrict the Reading of Young People," Worldandi.com, 2003,<http://www.worldandi.com/newhome/public/2003/september/mt2pub.asp> (October 15, 2005).

12. Foerstel, p. 202.

13. Ibid., p. 226.

14. Ibid.

Chapter 9.
Book Lovers Fight Back

1. Robert Cormier, "A Book Is Not a House: The Human Side of Censorship," in *Censorship: A Threat to Reading, Learning, Thinking* (Newark, Del.: International Reading Association, 1994), p. 62.

2. ReLeah Lent and Gloria Pipkin, "We Keep Pedaling," *The ALAN Review*, vol. 28, no. 2, 2001, <http://scholar.lib.vt.edu/ejournals/ALAN/v28n2/lent.html> (March 23, 2007).

3. Joan Vos MacDonald, *J. K. Rowling: Banned, Challenged, and Censored* (Berkeley Heights, N.J.: Enslow Publishers, Inc., 2008), p. 126.

4. Craig Lancto, "Banned Books: How Schools Restrict the Reading of Young People," Worldandi.com, 2003, <http://www.worldandi.com/newhome/public/2003/september/mt2pub.asp> (October 15, 2005).

5. E-mail from Margaret Sacco to author, April 24, 2006.

6. Letter from Renée (Cormier) Wheeler to author, April 2, 2006.

7. "1991 Margaret A. Edwards Award Winner," Young Adult Library Services Association, n.d., <http://www.ala.org/ala/yalsa/booklistsawards/margaretaedwards/maeprevious/1991awardwinner.htm> (July 2, 2007).

8. "1991 Margaret A. Edwards Award Winner," American Library Association/Young Adult Library

Services Association, 1991, <http://www.ala.org/ala/yalsa/booklistsawards/margaretaedwards/maeprevious/1991awardwinner.cfm> (February 12, 2008).

9. Telephone interview with B. A. "Tony" King, March 23, 2007.

Chapter 10.
Beyond the Twentieth Century

1. "Amelia V. Gallucci-Cirio Library: Robert E. Cormier Collection," Fitchburg State College Library, n.d., <http://www.fsc.edu/library/cormier2.html> (July 2, 2007).

2. Telephone interview with B. A. "Tony" King, March 23, 2007.

3. Letter to Fabio Coen from Robert Cormier, June 4, 1973, Robert Cormier Collection, Amelia V. Gallucci-Cirio Library, Fitchburg State College.

4. Letter to Fabio Coen from Robert Cormier, June 24, 1973, Robert Cormier Collection, Amelia V. Gallucci-Cirio Library, Fitchburg State College.

5. Letter from Fabio Coen to Robert Cormier, October 26, 1973, Robert Cormier Collection, Amelia V. Gallucci-Cirio Library, Fitchburg State College.

6. Interview with Robert Foley, November 17, 2005.

7. Robert Cormier obituary, *Independent*, November 8, 2000, p. 6, Amelia V. Gallucci-Cirio Library: Robert E. Cormier Collection, <http://www.fsc.edu/library/cormier2.html> (June 24, 2006).

8. Patty Campbell, *Robert Cormier: Daring to Disturb the Universe* (New York: Random House, 2006), p.1.

9. Letter from Bobbie (Cormier) Sullivan to author, April 2, 2006.

10. Telephone interview with B.A. "Tony" King, March 23, 2007.

11. ReLeah Lent and Gloria Pipkin, "We Keep Pedaling," *The ALAN Review*, vol. 28, no. 2, 2001, <http://scholar.lib.vt.edu/ejournals/ALAN/v28n2/lent.html> (March 23, 2007).

12. Robert Cormier, "Those Who Don't Make Headlines," *I Have Words to Spend: Reflections of a Small-Town Editor*, Constance Senay Cormier, ed. (New York: Bantam Doubleday Dell, 1991). Originally published in the *Fitchburg Sentinel and Enterprise*, October 31, 1972.

Published works of Robert Cormier

1960   *Now and at the Hour* (adult)

1963   *A Little Raw on Monday Mornings* (adult)

1965   *Take Me Where the Good Times Are* (adult)

1974   *The Chocolate War* (young adult)

1977   *I Am the Cheese* (young adult)

1979   *After the First Death* (young adult)

1980   *8 Plus 1: Stories*

1983   *The Bumblebee Flies Anyway* (young adult)

1985   *Beyond the Chocolate War* (young adult)

1988   *Fade* (young adult)

1990   *Other Bells for Us to Ring* (young adult)

1991   *We All Fall Down* (young adult)

1991   *I Have Words to Spend: Confessions of a Small-Town Editor* (adult, memoir)

1992   *Tunes for Bears to Dance To* (young adult)

1995   *In the Middle of the Night* (young adult)

1997   *Tenderness* (young adult)

1998   *Heroes* (young adult)

1999   *Frenchtown Summer* (young adult)

2000   *Portrait of a Parish* (adult)

2001   *The Rag and Bone Shop* (young adult; published posthumously)

Glossary

allusion—An indirect reference to another piece of literature or event.

carbon copy—A copy made with a piece of carbon paper between two sheets of typing paper as the letter was being typed. This method was typically used to make copies before personal computers came into popularity in the mid-1980s.

chilling effect—A situation where communication is hampered because of the fear of being punished.

epigraph—A quotation at the beginning of a literary work that suggests its theme.

metaphor—A comparison between unrelated things without using "like" or "as."

precautionary censorship—For the purposes of this book, when a librarian or teacher does not select a book in order to avoid conflict.

point of view—The persepective from which a story is told.

pseudonym—A pen name used by a writer, different from his or her real name.

Glossary

self-censorship—The situation occurring when a writer chooses not to write something because she or he thinks it will cause trouble.

simile—A comparison between unrelated things using "like" or "as."

theme—An idea that appears repeatedly throughout a story.

three-decker—A three-story tenement apartment house with many families living in it.

For More Information

The American Library Association
50 East Huron Street
Chicago, Ill. 60611
Telephone: 800-545-2433

Citizens for Community Values
11175 Reading Road, Suite 103
Cincinnati, Ohio 45241
Telephone: 513-733-5775
Fax: 513-733-5794

Focus on the Family
8605 Explorer Drive
Colorado Springs, Colo. 80920
Telephone: 1-800-A-FAMILY (1-800-232-6459)

International Reading Association
800 Barksdale Road, PO Box 8139
Newark, Del. 19714-8139
Telephone: 1-800-336-READ or 302-731-1600

National Council of Teachers of English
1111 W. Kenyon Road
Urbana, Ill. 61801-1096
Telephone: 1-800-369-6283 or 217-328-3870

Further Reading

Doyle, Robert P. *Banned Books*. Chicago: American Library Association, 2004.

Foerstel, Herbert. *Banned in the U.S.A.: A Reference Guide to Book Censorship in Schools and Public Libraries*. Westport, Conn.: Greenwood Press, 2002.

Hyde, Margaret O. *Robert Cormier*. Philadelphia: Chelsea House Publishers, 2005.

Karolides, Nicholas J., Margaret Bald, and Dawn B. Sova. *120 Banned Books: Censorship Histories of World Literature*. New York: Checkmark Books, 2005.

McPherson, Stephanie Sammartino. *Tinker v. Des Moines and Students' Right to Free Speech*. Berkeley Heights, NJ.: Enslow Publishers, Inc., 2006.

Ravitch, Diane. *The Language Police: How Pressure Groups Restrict What Students Learn*. New York: Knopf, 2003.

Thomson, Sarah L. *Robert Cormier*. New York: Rosen, 2003.

Internet Addresses

The American Library Association
<http://www.ala.org/>

Focus on the Family
<http://www.family.org>

Author Profile: Robert Cormier
<http://www.teenreads.com/authors/au-cormier-robert.asp>

Index

Index